HE and SHE

S. Carl Hirsch

HE and SHE

How Males and Females Behave

Illustrated by William Steinel

J. B. Lippincott Company
Philadelphia and New York

U.S. Library of Congress Cataloging in Publication Data

Hirsch, S   Carl.
  He and she: how males and females behave.

  Bibliography: p.
  Includes index.
  SUMMARY: Examines and compares the differences and similarities in the
behavior patterns of the male and female in various animal species including
human beings.
  1. Sexual behavior in animals — Juvenile literature. 2. Sex role — Juvenile
literature. 3. Animals, Habits and behavior of — Juvenile literature. [1. Animals — Habits and behavior. 2. Sex role] I. Steinel, William L. II. Title.
QL761.H57   591.5'6   75-15983
ISBN-0-397-31633-X

For the Astrup family,
our gracious Zululand hosts.

Author's Acknowledgments

To Margaret Mead I am deeply indebted for a close, critical reading of the text. Her perceptive comments have guided me through a number of difficulties, particularly in the writing of the last chapter.

The manuscript has had the benefit of evaluation and examination by a number of leading scientists in animal behavior and related fields. I would like to thank Prof. John Alcock, Department of Zoology, Arizona State University; Prof. Alexander Alland, Jr., Department of Anthropology, Columbia University; Prof. Peter Klopfer, Zoology Department, Duke University; Prof. David Pilbeam, Department of Anthropology, Yale University.

For his time and wisdom I would like to thank Prof. Harry F. Harlow, for many years the Director of the Primate Research Center at the University of Wisconsin. At the same institution Prof. D. A. Goldfoot and John Wolf were extremely helpful.

My visit to the home and laboratory of Karl von Frisch in Austria was enriched by hours spent with Galatea Frisch, the niece of the renowned scientist and his co-worker for many years. At the Max Planck Institut für Verhaltensphysiologie, my informative escort was Fritz Trillmich, at that time a doctoral candidate in animal behavior.

I am also grateful to: Dr. George Rabb of the Brookfield (Illinois) Zoo for points of information; Lois Hansen and her classes in Lincoln, Nebraska, where some of the ideas herein were discussed with students; George Hödlmoser of St. Gilgen, Austria, a friend of the family of Karl von Frisch.

The "we" of the narrative is myself and Stina L. Hirsch, my wife and my associate in the research and technical work on this book.

Contents

1·The Two Sexes

—Female fireflies do flash, but do not fly.

—In the sea catfish family, it is father who cares for and carries the eggs — in his mouth.

—Any mosquito who stings will surely be a she.

—The pheasant sporting the gaudiest of feathered finery is certainly not the female of the species.

—A bullfrog heard croaking in the pond may be a member of either sex — but the chirping cricket is definitely a male.

—The "lone" he-wolf is seldom alone and is usually a highly devoted mate and parent.

—In a hive of bees, the females do all the work, and the males do all the loafing.

Do such homely facts about animal social and family life seem strange? They are — if creatures in the wild are thought to behave like people. Or if we expect people to behave like animals. Or if we believe nature has put all males and females neatly into prearranged roles that are firm and fixed everywhere and forever.

Some primitive forms of life have no clear-cut sexuality. But generally, animal species have evolved two sexes, at most. This simple fact has made life enormously complex, endlessly changeful and often quite bewildering.

In order to understand animal life, it is not enough simply to observe the various species and their activities. Animals must also be seen as males and females, as they behave separately and together, from birth through adulthood.

No two species act alike. No two individuals behave exactly the same. In fact, the habits of animals are so varied that there may seem to be no commonness at all. As we look at the full array of the earth's living species, the males and females present us with an astonishing range of behaviors.

And yet, we painstakingly gather information about their relationships. We search for an orderly pattern. Somewhere there must be a way of understanding sexual behaviors, which in turn hold clues to natural selection.

In what ways are the males and females of a species similar? In what ways different? How do they meet and mate? What parts do the two sexes play in the activities of pairing, nesting, providing food and nurturing for the young? How do the individuals of each species act toward members of the same and of the opposite sex?

And somewhere, half-hidden in all of our questions, is an anxious one: What does the study of such animal behavior tell us about ourselves as human beings — if anything?

Run in pursuit of these questions and you may find yourself caught up by them. They become fascinating. Perhaps you will undertake the search for answers as a scientist or scholar. Or else you may be among the curious amateurs urged on by the lure of a mystery as large as life.

One can follow the single wilderness track of a naturalist. Or peer over the shoulder of the experimental biologist at the dissecting table. Or perhaps stare for long periods at a cageful of doves, as instruments record how many times they perform certain acts. There are almost unlimited ways to study animal behavior.

My wife and I have camped in the African habitat of the so-called white rhino and joined a research team observing prairie dog coteries in Kansas. We have gone from the quaint Austrian mountain village of St. Gilgen to the quiet corridors of England's Oxford University to a nature reserve in Bavaria — all in the footsteps of three men who won the Nobel Prize for their studies of animal behavior. And we have spent days on a college campus among a huge population of nonhuman primates. These are only a few of the countless places where the behavior of living things is under close scrutiny.

The bodies of animals have been studied for centuries. There exists a rich treasury of knowledge about the bones and muscles, the fur and fins, the organs and tissues of uncounted existing species and many that are now extinct. But study of their behavior as living creatures is fairly recent. There is not yet a stock of solid information about how a great many species conduct their private lives.

It will not be surprising, then, to learn that not all scientists in this field agree. Many fundamental questions about animal behavior are still under hot debate. As for the behavior of males and females, that subject often stirs strong feelings — even among scientists. There are long-standing opinions about how the members of both sexes "naturally" behave. Some of these notions go back thousands of years.

Scientists today use symbols for the two sexes: ♂ means male; ♀ means female.

Oddly, these symbols come out of the ancient belief in astrology, which has no connection whatsoever with modern science. Astrology is based on the idea that heavenly bodies control the lives of human beings and determine their behavior.

The astrological symbol for male has the form of a spear carrier. It represents Mars, the bringer of war.

The female symbol is that of Venus. She is represented as a lovesick beauty, forever gazing into her looking glass.

In the Middle Ages, the alchemists gave these two symbols still other uses. ♂ came to represent steel, the *hard* metal from which swords were forged. ♀ stood for copper, the *soft* metal from which containers were fashioned.

These images of the male and the female are typical of age-old beliefs about the two sexes which persist to this day in Western cultures. Supposedly males are "by nature" brave, active, practical and aggressive; females are said to be vain, fearful, passive and subservient.

The Greek philosopher Aristotle compiled many of the popular opinions that had been formed up to his time about the nature of living beings. He seemed to see differing patterns of temperament and behavior in the sexes — among animals and human beings. "Everywhere in nature, the male stands above the female," he asserted, claiming that males were superior in every way. As for humankind, he added: "The courage of men is shown in commanding; the courage of women is in obeying."

While such ancient ideas were questioned at times in the distant past, they were probably never seriously challenged, nor put to a conclusive test. Unproven, they formed the basis for customs, laws, religious practices and social habits of many human societies. Thus they took on the semblance of truth.

In the same way, a great many other beliefs about behavior patterns became deeply implanted in human thought and culture. Behavior was held to be under the control of mysterious inner forces. People and animals supposedly acted according to their "inborn nature."

Across the centuries, people have believed that all living things, including human beings, were largely governed by a set of fixed and unchanging impulses. Supposedly, individuals, groups and whole societies were locked into predetermined patterns of conduct. People and animals were said to be driven by "natural instincts" for hoarding, herding, fighting, mothering, mating, homing, competing, killing, seeking possessions, power and dominance.

It is only in recent times that such ideas about behavior have been seriously questioned. Less than a century ago Charles Darwin made the first systematic and scientific efforts to get to the roots of animal behavior. His ideas began modern biology. Darwin revealed how species are formed. He also offered clues as to why they behave as they do.

The finch, as Charles Darwin knew it, was a small, drab type of bird with a pleasing call, well known to British gardeners and farmers because of its insect- and seed-eating habits.

The finches that Darwin found in the Galápagos Islands in the year 1835 were quite a surprise. They were different from the British finches in two ways — in the shapes of their beaks and in their eating habits. The voyaging young naturalist noted a "most curious fact" — that their varied feeding behaviors on different islands had resulted in the formation of thirteen distinct species.

On each of the Galápagos Islands, finches had found new

GALAPAGOS FINCHES

INSECT EATER

WARBLER FINCH

PLANT EATER

VEGETARIAN TREE FINCH

PLANT AND INSECT EATERS

WOODPECKER FINCH (TOOL-USING)

MANGROVE FINCH

SMALL INSECTIVOROUS
TREE FINCH

LARGE INSECTIVOROUS
TREE FINCH

MEDIUM INSECTIVOROUS
TREE FINCH

SHARP-BEAKED
GROUND FINCH

LARGE CACTUS
GROUND FINCH

CACTUS GROUND FINCH

MEDIUM GROUND FINCH

LARGE GROUND FINCH

SMALL GROUND FINCH

habitats and sources of food. Over many generations, those surviving finches best adapted to these new habitats had handed down to their offspring the special traits which better fitted them for their living conditions. In this way, the beaks of the finches had become differentiated. Some were best suited for nut-cracking, others for fly-catching or sap-sucking or cactus-eating or other uses.

As Darwin put it, "One species had been taken and modified for different ends." Such thinking was to give rise to Darwin's theory of natural selection, which overturned the biology of the past. However, the theory explained more than how species change in form. Darwin also suggested how natural selection works to bring animal behavior patterns into being.

Animal habits do not come about through an act of will or a moment's whim. The most casual observer of animals can see that they behave in ways that are specifically suited to the conditions of their lives. The minnow travels in a school even though it does not have the intelligence to figure out the advantages of doing so. A bird does not know its song is functional. The squirrel storing nuts is unable to plan ahead to its needs of the coming winter. The nesting eagle is not conscious of what is inside the egg which it incubates. And yet, such useful behaviors are as typical of species as the color of a wren's eggs or the size of a baboon's teeth or the shape of a beetle's wings.

Many early observers of animals pointed out that typical behaviors were linked to advantages in reproduction. But there was no clear understanding of the origin of behavior patterns until after 1859, when Charles Darwin offered an explanation for natural selection.

In Darwin's view, the inhabitants of the earth are survivors of an endless process of sifting and screening. In each of the uncounted generations past, a great many of those born did not survive and their individual traits died with them. However, those born with traits especially useful for living in their own environment and reproducing young not only survived, they lived to produce numerous offspring, who inherited these same useful traits. In this way, entire species have in time become well adapted to their living environments.

Through such adaptations, the salamander acquired its long, darting tongue, the sloth its branch-gripping hand, the gull a wing shaped for soaring, the camel a series of special features useful for life in the desert. Did the same process of development also provide these animals with the behaviors that accompany these physical features?

Charles Darwin did not directly apply his principle of natural selection to animal habits. He had no evidence that proved behavior can be inherited — as is the color of an eye or the shape of a claw. And yet, patterns of conduct useful for survival clearly reappeared in each species from one generation to the next.

In his late years of life, Darwin continued to mull the mysteries of behavior. He marveled at how clearly mammals could express fear, grief, anger, surprise, joy and affection, communicating these emotions in a variety of ways. He also developed what he called the principle of "service" to explain the formation of habits. Such behaviors, he said, "are of direct or indirect service to relieve or gratify certain sensations, desires." The British biologist was suggesting a way of viewing animal behavior — applying to it the test of usefulness.

Darwin also looked deeply into the behavior of males and females, seeking patterns in the pairing of animals. He developed a theory of what he called "sexual selection" which probed the manner in which animals choose their mates.

However, this remained after Darwin's death among his many ideas that were yet to be proved and accepted. His theories continued to stir fiery arguments both in and out of the scientific world. And at the end of the nineteenth century, many of the noted scientists of the world were not "Darwinians." One of those who remained unconvinced was a Frenchman, Jean Henri Fabre — a man whom Darwin admired as "an incomparable observer."

2 · "Little People"

In the south of France there is a tangled garden where the spiders have noted ancestors. These eight-leggers are descended through many generations from the spiders that were studied by the naturalist Jean Henri Fabre.

His house is still there. A pull on the bell chain brings a caretaker who will open the garden gate. Few visitors find their way to this old homestead on the edge of the languid village of Serignan. Today Fabre is well known mainly by children who still read his delightful tales and by those scientists who are aware that he made the first serious studies of insect behavior.

In this house he lived and worked for thirty-five years until his death in 1915. This is no grand museum. It is hardly recognizable as the laboratory of one who opened new scientific fields. We wandered here in the footsteps of a pleasant and modest man who lived frugally on foods that he grew himself, read but little, owned not so much as a simple microscope, acquired his insect specimens through the open window and was aided by a cheerful staff of his own children.

"The secrets of life are revealed," Fabre wrote, "to those who use the simplest implements, tools improvised for the occasion and costing nothing."

By today's standards, Fabre's observations lacked precision and his experiments were crude. But for vivid description of the behaviors of male and female insects, Fabre is still unmatched. There is poetry as well as science in his writings. And for blood-chilling drama, read his accounts of how the hunting wasp instantly puts her prey into a deadly coma, or how the scorpion deals violently with its mate.

In his study is the tiny writing desk he used for a lifetime, a homemade butterfly net, letters he never answered (including one from Charles Darwin), just a few preserved insects, since he was never an avid collector. Around the large table in the center of the room is a track worn into the tile floor where Fabre paced round and round, encircling his own puzzled thoughts.

Revealing much about the curious life he lived are the two unkempt acres around the house, the tangled garden with its frog pond, the weedy thickets of shrubs and brambles, the fallow fields — all shrewdly calculated as a haven for the assorted insects of the neighborhood. To his fellow townsfolk, who sometimes peered over the high garden wall, it seemed that Fabre had fenced in a piece of chaotic wilderness. But this was his dream place. He bought it toward the end of a toilsome life. He had long wished for such "an abandoned, barren, sun-scorched bit of land, favored by thistles and by wasps and bees."

Here he clumped about in his wooden peasant shoes, wearing a linen jacket and a black broad-brimmed hat. He was a small man, shrunken in his old age, his face thin-cheeked and deep-lined, the long gray hair falling in wispy curls. His dark eyes shone with unusual depth and brilliance. And he expressed himself volubly like a true peasant of Provence, gesturing, arguing, chuckling, bursting with delight over his latest finds.

The gentle Fabre lured his entire family, his wife and eight children, into the insect habitats with him. They shared his enthusiasm. And the children invited their friends from the village as willing co-workers. They brought unusual live specimens for study and joined in the fascination of observing. Fabre soberly paid them each for their labor — with a sugarplum, a coin, a piece of bread and honey.

"Inspector of spider webs," Fabre called himself. And what a wonder-struck group he had with him watching by lantern light a common garden spider spinning its flat, circular web. Night after night in late July they gathered after dark to observe the Epeira's construction. Entranced, they saw the web being joined out of what appeared to be moonbeams. The long radial lines were spun out, then overlaid with spiral tracery to complete the female spider's food-gathering trap. "What refinement of art for a mess of flies!" Fabre cried out.

The younger members of the family often had to be in bed before the orb was completed. "Has she finished yet?" the children would call softly through the windows. "Has she caught a moth?"

Through Fabre's vivid account the reader becomes absorbed, drawn into the present moment of what is happening on an August night. From the nearby bushes, a male spider appears. He is tiny compared to the web-spinning female. Clearly his object is mating. But how hesitantly he approaches his mate! He climbs in short spurts, backing off quickly whenever the female makes a move.

Fabre explains to his family in whispers about the male of the species. He is a rare visitor to the web, this under-sized dwarf. Compared to the female of this species, he has little talent for hunting; he offers no protection for his offspring, spins no webs, does not nurture the young, lives a short, uneventful life and is usually dead before the eggs are laid. His one important act, mating, is a perilous one. Unless he is clearly identified by the female, he is in great danger of being mistaken for prey. His nervous movements on the web cable may rouse the huntress to action and he could be quickly eaten alive.

Many years after Fabre's research, scientists would show that the male spider has his own system for vibrating the line, thereby establishing his identity as a friendly mate. But the signals are by no means foolproof, as the high death rate of males shows.

On this night in Serignan, however, the tiny male sur-vives and the speedy mating act is completed. As Fabre recounts: "The object of the expedition is attained. The whipper-snapper makes off at full speed, as though he had the Furies at his heels. If he remained, he would presuma-bly be eaten. These exercises on the tightrope are not repeated. I kept watch in vain on the following evenings. I never saw the fellow again."

Fabre was a time-biding, strong-willed man who waited almost a lifetime to begin the career he wanted from the first. Observing insects was a passion with him. But noth-ing in his family background gave the slightest hint that this would be his life's work.

His people were poor, plain, unschooled. An insect to them was a pest to be crushed underfoot. And more than once he was cuffed on the head for his idleness when he gathered up insects in order to watch their behavior. "There is nothing in my heredity to explain my taste for observation," Fabre remarked. He was sent to live with his grandparents during his childhood, spending his early years in "a lean farm on a cold granite ridge." There, as a gentle and lonely child, he first sought the company of beetles and moths and spiders. Throughout a long lifetime, he retained a view of them as "little people," oddly formed, possessed of bewildering skills, astonishing in their behavior.

By unflagging effort he acquired an education and became a poorly paid teacher in the French schools. As a middle-aged professor, he earned hardly as much as the local stableboy.

A single desire haunted him. He wanted only to have a tiny bit of wilderness of his own. How content he would be to spend his days among the free-living insects he knew so well! However, the chances for such a life looked unpromising. The meager income of a teacher would not buy even the poorest of acres. The prospect of retiring to any place but the poorhouse was dim indeed. There was no possibility that anyone would be paid a salary in those mid-nineteenth-century years for studying the behavior of dung beetles and mayflies!

As a science teacher in the town of Avignon, Fabre began in the late 1860s a series of free evening lectures. He was trying to reach a broader audience than that in his classroom. He opened these lectures to young women — something unheard of! By rigid tradition, the higher education of women in France was entirely in the hands of the clergy. Careers in science were not open to women, nor were they permitted to glimpse worlds beyond church and kitchen, nursery and sickroom.

For his daring effort, Fabre was denounced as a dangerous man who was tampering with age-old rules that had put the female of the human species in her place. He was dismissed from his teaching post and his family was evicted from their lodgings.

It was a time of great despair for the aging naturalist. He now turned to writing booklets for children. Here his talents shone. These writings sought to give children a taste for science, not by reciting dull facts but by stimulating their curiosity, stirring his readers to discover for themselves truths about the natural world.

His booklets were written with simplicity and charm. Would the reader like to see how the earth moves? Then pierce a slice of dry bread with a sharpened twig; and now, twirling this top, observe how a planet travels through space. Some principles of physics were illustrated through the use of a popgun. And Fabre instructed his readers how they could hollow out an apricot stone, equip it with two straws and set it to work siphoning water.

The books were a modest success. And now at last, in his late fifties, Fabre could see glimmering a chance for the postponed career of his yearnings. Perhaps he had waited too long. "I greatly fear," he remarked, "that the peach is offered to me when I am beginning to have no teeth with which to eat it."

With his so-called retirement, Fabre's new life commenced. The overgrown acres he bought at Serignan became his "great museum of the fields." He had no need to look for the subjects of his study; they came to him day and night, in every season, in successive generations, in all stages of their development, exhibiting the full range of their natural behaviors.

On a May morning, a huge moth broke from her cocoon, weakly fluttered her damp wings. That day ended with what Fabre called "the Great Peacock evening." Let him describe the scene:

"At nine o'clock in the evening, just as the household is going to bed, there is a great stir in the room next to mine.

Little Paul, half-undressed, is rushing about, jumping and
stamping, knocking the chairs over like a mad thing. I hear
him call to me:

"'Come quick!' he screams. 'Come and see these moths,
big as birds. The room is full of them!'

"I hurry in. There is enough to justify the child's enthusiastic exclamations — an invasion as yet unprecedented
in our house, a raid of giant moths."

Now Fabre remembers the newborn female moth caged
in a jar downstairs. He and young Paul clatter down to the
study with its large open windows.

"We enter the room, candle in hand. What we see is
unforgettable. With a soft flick-flack the great moths fly
around the jar, alight, set off again, come back, fly up to the

ceiling and down. They rush at the candle, putting it out with a stroke of their wings; they descend on our shoulders, clinging to our clothes, grazing our faces. The scene suggests a wizard's cave, with its whirl of bats. Little Paul holds my hand tighter than usual, to keep up his courage."

The Great Peacock moths, spectacular in their coloring, velvety, their wings each marked with a big staring eye, are known everywhere in the world. But rarely are they seen in large numbers. How account for the mass invasion of the Fabre household?

Undoubtedly, the young female trapped in Fabre's study was drawing troops of male moths. But as a census taker of insect populations, Fabre knew at once that such a numerous assembly could only be drawn from a vast area and from long distances. What signal could have brought them so far?

In the next few nights, Fabre eliminated the possibility that the female might have been seen by the males. Trees and a wall surrounded the house, and Fabre further cut off visibility by moving the caged female to a part of the house away from windows. But after dark each night for a week the pursuing males appeared.

By a series of additional experiments, Fabre could only come to the conclusion that the males were attracted by an odor, picked up on their feathery antennae, which are sensitive organs of smell. Like many other mating signals in the animal world, this one was not perceptible to human senses. It remained for scientists who came long after Fabre to verify that it is indeed a faint scent that brings together male and female moths. In recent years, the chemical substance that produces this smell has been identified in the laboratory.

To Fabre the case of the Great Peacock moth was one more adventure in his search for what he called the "instincts" of insects. He carefully distinguished his work from that of professional scientists in those years who were absorbed entirely by the anatomy and the chemistry of animals. And in moments of bitterness, he cried out against narrow-minded biologists who could see no value in studying the behavior of living things.

"You rip up the animal and I study it alive," Fabre wrote. "You turn it into an object of horror and pity, whereas I cause it to be loved. You labor in torture-chamber and dissecting-room; I make my observations under the blue sky. You subject cell and protoplasm to chemical tests; I study instinct in its loftiest manifestations. You pry into death, I pry into life!"

His major work during the years at Serignan was ten volumes which he called *Studies in the Instincts and Habits of the Insects*. Original information taken from his own observations in the field filled these books. They covered a wide range of species, relating in great detail how insects carry on their daily lives. The books were written in everyday language, but the scientific accuracy of most of his accounts has never been challenged. They were set down in the spirit of wonder and open admiration.

He was struck by the skills of the hunting wasp. And he spent hours watching the female as she overpowered her prey. Fabre offered the wasp a male grasshopper, only to have it rejected. It took him a while to understand that the hunting wasp needed a particular kind of food for her hungry larvae.

"The wasp would have nothing to say to my game," Fabre wrote. "'A male, indeed! Is that a dinner for my larvae? What do you take them for?'" The naturalist noted how well the wasp seeking prey could distinguish "between the tender flesh of an egg-bearing female and the comparatively dry flesh of the males."

But now Fabre watched closely as the hunting wasp revealed the most astounding of her tricks. These wasps are themselves nourished only by the nectar of flowers; but their larvae are meat-eaters, feeding on the flesh and body juices of live insects. How was the wasp to bring home its captive alive?

Instead of stinging her prey with a poisonous barb, the wasp puts her victim into deep sleep by pressing at a certain point on its skull! "Without ever being taught or seeing it practiced by others, she understands her surgery through and through," Fabre wrote. "She knows the most delicate mysteries of the physiology of the nerves, or rather behaves as if she did. She knows that under her victim's brain there is a circlet of nervous nuclei and that compression here will cause all resistance to cease." The prey is dragged home paralyzed. The larvae feast on fresh meat for a week or two while the victim is slowly dying not of its wounds but of starvation.

Fabre marveled at what he saw in his wild park. The insects exhibited habits that made them appear sometimes as skilled craftsmen or as creators of art works or as wizards who planned their lives with intelligence and foresight. But he saw also that their mentality was very limited.

"Their instincts are absolutely without reasoning power, notwithstanding the wonderful perfection of their work," he wrote. "They build, weave, hunt in the same way as they digest their food, without the least understanding of the means or the end. They are, I am convinced, completely ignorant of their own wonderful talents."

Fabre was baffled by the habits of these creatures. At one moment an army of ants might be carrying out a marvelous cross-country expedition. But should something new appear in their path, they were unable to cope with it, and the work abruptly ceased. He noted how incapable a spider was of repairing a damaged web or a moth of patching a torn cocoon. On the other hand, certain habits seemed to persist so stubbornly that almost nothing could stop their occurrence.

Could anything halt for even a moment the cicada's endless crackle? Fabre tried shouting, clattering pans and setting off fireworks — without results. Finally he persuaded the local militia to wheel its two ancient cannons into his garden. The blasts shocked the country folk speechless. But the cicadas in the trees continued merrily without a moment's interruption. Fabre could only conclude that the cicadas were deaf — or at least hard of hearing. But it was for him one more example of the kind of insect behavior that seems to go its merry mindless way, whatever else may intervene.

"The insect which astounds, which terrifies us with its extraordinary intelligence, surprises us in the next moment with its stupidity when confronted with some simple fact that happens to lie outside its ordinary practice," Fabre observed.

The naturalist paced his study into the late hours, pondering the mysteries of what he continued to call "instinct." How explain the habits of insects, or those of other animals? And in what ways could these behaviors be compared to those of human beings?

Fabre understood well that the mentality of his "little people" was quite different from that of human beings. And yet he could not forgive them for their "improper" behavior.

The naturalist was in some ways a rebel. But he was also a respectable French villager who lived according to the customs of his people, accepted the ideas of his society, the morals of his age. And he frowned on insect behavior that fell short of these standards.

Did not insect predators spread terror among the weak? And bee colonies destroy their own disabled larvae? And were not creatures inclined at times to eat their young? Fabre shook his head in dismay. "There it is in all its horror — the right of might," he wrote. "Man did the same in days of old: he stripped and ate his fellows. We continue to rob one another, both as nations and as individuals, but we no longer eat one another."

He was like a kindly, affectionate uncle, often talking directly to the insects, chiding them for their waywardness. To Fabre they included the bright and the stupid, the gentle and the violent, the virtuous and the evil — even as in human society. "Here, as among us," he wrote, "are honest toilers and free-booters, producers and parasites, good and bad husbands and wives; examples of beautiful devotion and hideous egoism; delightful amenities and ferocious cruelties, extending even to cannibalism; workers of every class and manufacturers of every kind."

The habits of some insect males and females he found especially shameful. What he observed in his own garden seemed to be shocking behavior for his peasant village, with its stolid, hardworking men and its pious, black-shawled women. In speaking of the intimate lives of insects, Fabre used such terms as "orgies" and "perverse lusts" and "bestial delights."

Probably the praying mantis distressed him most. This insect is commonly seen with its forelimbs raised in what appears to be an attitude of worship. Fabre charged that "these pious airs conceal the most atrocious habits."

It was bad enough that the mantis was a voracious meat-eater, feeding exclusively on living prey. But Fabre was appalled by the mating habits of the female. He described the mantis pair in the sexual act. "The male, absorbed in the performance of his vital functions, holds the female in a tight embrace." Then in horror Fabre reported what ensued: "But the wretch has no head; he has no neck; he has hardly a body. The other continues very placidly to gnaw what remains of the gentle swain. And all the time that masculine stump, holding on firmly, goes on with the business!"

Fabre could tolerate some questionable behavior among

mating insects, "but gobbling him up during the act goes beyond the wildest dreams of the most horrible imagination." He added: "I have seen it done with my own eyes and have not yet recovered from my astonishment."

This student of "instinct" had no way of explaining "such evil conduct by one of God's own creatures." Fabre was himself a deeply religious man with a view of the world that came directly from the Scriptures. According to that view, living beings were little changed from the moment when all had suddenly appeared on the newly created earth. Supposedly their behaviors were part of their total beings. How then could one understand the cruelty and lust, the greed and ferocity which Fabre seemed to see in the "instincts" of animals? In despair, he envisioned nature as "a savage foster-mother who knows nothing of pity." How could all this have been included in the Divine Plan?

Fabre was out of touch with his fellow scientists who had already accepted Darwin's theory that all animal species were ever-changing, that all had sprung from a common origin, developing in their separate ways through natural selection. Fabre paid little attention to these explosive advances in biological science. The naturalist in Provence could not bring himself to read more than a few pages of Darwin's *On the Origin of Species*. For a man with his religious views there could be no question as to how species originated. He believed devoutly that the insects he now studied had first appeared along with all the rest of the animal kingdom on the fifth day of Creation.

At times his research had offered him startling evidence that species do change, responding to new conditions in their environment. But the whole idea of evolution was alien to him, not only challenging his deepest religious beliefs but seeming to turn life into a wild and chaotic gamble, without control or order.

How could the random processes of natural selection

bring about the harmony which he saw in nature? It seemed to Fabre that the theory of evolution merely depicted "a long list of casual experiments." How could the workings of a "game of chance" ever explain the complex social life of ants, or the spider weaving its magnificent web?

3 · Dancers, Drones and Dowagers

In the summer of 1913, a bright young Austrian biologist, Karl von Frisch, began his first serious studies of the senses of animals. Unlike Fabre, he saw nothing "casual" or "chaotic" about natural selection.

For von Frisch, Darwin's theory not only accounted for the physical forms of the various species, it also explained their habits. Their behaviors were the responses of living things to their surrounding world, a world perceived through their senses. Physical forms, behaviors, sensory organs — all were adaptations for survival.

Was it reasonable to suppose, he wondered, that fishes, which need to find certain other fishes in order to reproduce, have no senses of smell or hearing? Or that honeybees, which have a life-and-death relationship with flowers, are color-blind? Scientists had "proved" the absence of these sensory faculties. And who was Karl von Frisch, only recently finished with his schooling and still in his twenties, to challenge these learned opinions?

He was a small, wiry fellow with a sharp chin and close-cropped hair. His own family circle in Vienna included noted professors, scientists, doctors — but Karl was not overawed by any of them. Brash, zealous, orderly-minded, he chose a career in biology, describing himself as "an enthusiastic Darwinian." In 1913, natural selection was still a fresh, new viewpoint from which to reexamine all the biological questions of the past. The challenge was to apply Darwin's theory to unsolved problems with new and boldly designed experiments.

Some of the experiments which had "proved" that fishes were deaf showed that they did not seem to react to a variety of sounds. Fishes were subjected to shrieks, blasts, horn solos and even the songs of an operatic soprano. They didn't seem to hear a thing.

To Karl von Frisch it seemed that the fishes had been given no incentives to pass these tests. "Now, if I were a fish . . ." he said to himself. His reasoning led him to conclude that a fish might respond to the sound of a dinner bell — but only if accompanied by the dinner. For five days he trained a catfish by sounding a whistle call and offering it food at the same moment. On the sixth day, the catfish appeared out of the depths of its pond merely at the sound of Karl's summons!

The young biologist was elated. He attracted much attention with his first scientific paper, entitled "A Fish That Comes When One Whistles."

Encouraged toward further research projects on the senses of animals, Karl followed the wilderness paths that had intrigued him since his childhood. In a scenic region of Austria, amid towering Alps and shimmering lakes, his family owned property in a hamlet called Brunnwinkl. Karl had been coming here each summer for mountain climbing and hiking, for swimming and sailing on Lake Wolfgang.

He and his three older brothers, all excellent musicians, got together in Brunnwinkl to play music they loved, the string quartets of Haydn and Brahms. Young Karl was attracted too to the harmonies which he saw in nature. He marveled at the well-ordered life of the common honeybee.

For ages past, hive bees were admired not only for the honey they produced but also for their highly organized colonies. It was well known that their relationship with flowers supplied the bees with nectar. At the same time, the bees carried pollen on their bodies from blossom to blossom, thus aiding in the reproduction of flowers. Pollen grains are the male germ cells, which combine with the female cells or ovules commonly located at the petal base of flowers.

Karl found himself challenging the commonly held theory that bees could not distinguish one color from another. Was it believable, asked von Frisch, that colorful flowers, which depend for survival on bee pollenation, "should be nothing but a meaningless display before the eyes of color-blind insects?"

What blossomed in Brunnwinkl during that and the following years were myriad colored sheets of paper with which Karl tested the eyesight of bees. By distributing dishes of sugar water on backgrounds of some colors and dishes of plain water on others, the young biologist was able to show beyond question that bees were well aware of colors. In fact, their color sense enables bees to carry out one of their characteristic bits of behavior. Scout bees, which are specialized in foraging for food, are "flower constant," that is, each scout normally visits only the flowers of one species. Because it is drawn to a certain color, the bee is able to deliver to a flower the specific kind of pollen which is needed in order for that flower to propagate.

In the spring of 1919, von Frisch followed a food-gathering honeybee scout back to her home base. He adjusted his thick spectacles and strained to see into the murky hive. Through the dimness he watched a strange ritual. "I could scarcely believe my eyes," the biologist later reported.

For weeks he had been asking himself how it was that after a bee forager visited a place rich in foodstuff, scores of other bees from the same hive would quickly find their way to that same food source. Was there some signal by which the scout sent her hive mates to the find?

As von Frisch watched intently, the returning forager performed a kind of circular dance on the honeycomb, doubling back and forth, left and right, buzzing her wings. She was being closely followed by a train of other scouts, as though they were tracing the dancer's steps. Soon the cluster of scouts flew out, headed for the feeding place.

Von Frisch pondered the full meaning of what he had seen in the darkness of the hive. He later recalled: "This I believe was the most far-reaching observation of my life."

Each season spent with the bees of Brunnwinkl left him impatient to resume observation the following spring. He was now aware of the bee "spy system," but did not yet know exactly how it functioned — and the mystery gave him no rest. Again and again he watched the scout's circular dance, tracing its movements and directions, rhythm and tempo.

It was only when he lengthened by many meters the distance of his food offering from the hive that von Frisch detected something entirely new. The dance changed. With long flight distance to the target, the scout performed a waggle dance, shaking its body and whirring its wings, moving in a straight line, then veering off first to one side and then to the other.

What did it all mean? Perhaps the bees could fully understand the message, but von Frisch and his associates could not. They analyzed every part of the waggle dance without finding the answer they sought.

Then all at once the clues seemed to fall into place. Every bee movement had a meaning of its own. The distance of the food target was indicated by the rhythm of the dance. The direction was being shown in relation to the position of the sun. The bee code had been broken!

A guest in Brunnwinkl can readily understand how this place drew Karl von Frisch all the summers of his life. In June 1974, we came to this tiny, roadless hamlet to pay homage to its venerable scientist.

We sailed on its wind-rippled "sea," clambered on its rocky hills, tramped the biologist's bee runs. Von Frisch's spacious house is a one-time gristmill three hundred years old, its lower levels kept damp and cool in the summer by a mountain-fed millstream. In the attic we sat in his workroom amid the nature collections he has gathered since childhood.

In his late eighties, he was still rising at each day's dawn, to take exploratory walks which never failed to reveal to him some new bit of insight into plant and animal life. A little man dressed in Tyrolean garb, he still found delight in what he called "biology at its healthiest and best."

Why his keen, longtime interest in the senses of living things? And why does a scientist spend fifty years mainly studying one species? "Every single species of the animal kingdom challenges us with all, or nearly all, the mysteries of life," was his reply. The student of animal behavior carefully chooses an experimental animal and comes to know it exceedingly well, von Frisch added. He is then in a position to interpret many kinds of behavior, observed under a great variety of experimental conditions.

He could offer no better example than that of honeybees, whose amazing social behavior and communication could easily be mistaken for something which it is not. Von Frisch makes no claims of intelligence for his bees. In fact, he has made it very clear that bees show no reasoning power whatever when confronted with a situation different from the accustomed one.

Was bee behavior, then, purely a matter of instinct? Modern research has raised serious doubts as to whether innate forces in themselves determine the ways in which living things function. In this century, scientists have continued to argue not only about the power of instincts but also about the extent to which behavior patterns may be learned or affected by experiences or stimuli from the environment.

Von Frisch wisely avoided such debates, which be belived would probably never produce any new understanding. His work with bees convinced him that probably no one would ever determine what part of a worker bee's activity was fixed by its inheritance and what part was brought about by outside stimuli.

The biologist was too much of a Darwinian to accept the notion that anything in nature is unchangeable, least of all the behavior of animals. He had often observed that honeybees could learn to take on new work patterns within a certain range to meet changing needs within the hive. And in comparing the different ways in which living things form into varied social groups, he noted that "external conditions may be the favoring cause."

*

In nature there are few hermits. Animals seem to reach out for each other. A mated male and female are the most simple kind of social organization. The family is the next larger biological unit. And from such a base, a society may build to the size and complexity we see among human beings — or among bees.

In probing the inner life of the hive, Karl von Frisch learned the secrets of how a bee society functions. "The essential feature of a society is not the number of its members," he remarked, "but its inner organization."

The necessities and the routines of a society require some kind of communication among its members. In honeybees, the ability to exchange information essential to survival has been highly developed by a small insect with a brain the size of a pinhead.

The honeybee hive is a closed society — not a group of families but a single superfamily, uniting perhaps fifty thousand "blood relatives." The needs of the hive determine the behavior of males and females. And the colony functions like a well-run factory.

The important part of the hive structure is a network of homemade wax combs which is formed of a great many six-sided tubes. These are wax-sealed, food-filled cradles in which first the eggs, then the larvae develop. The outer combs are storage bins for food, which may be raided by humans and other animals for their honey.

In the hive, there is a strict separation of roles between the two sexes. The females known as workers are by far the largest part of the population. They toil ceaselessly at a succession of useful jobs, beginning very young as cleaners of the hive. Most of their entire lifetime of about six weeks is spent building, maintaining, repairing and guarding the hive, nursing the young, attending the queen. At last, they become scouts and foragers, ending their lives in the most demanding and dangerous of their tasks. The female worker bees have themselves been raised on

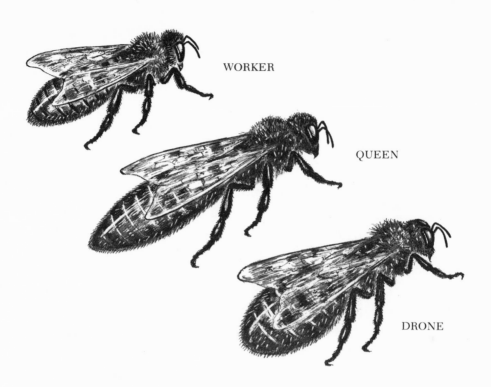

WORKER

QUEEN

DRONE

meager food supplies and in narrow cells so that they
never develop the ability to mate and lay eggs.

These sexual duties are performed only by a special type
of female, the so-called queen. In the hive, a female is
prepared for the queen's role and favored with extraordinary nourishment. She is also provided with roomy quarters in which to grow larger in size than any other member
of the colony. Since she is the only bee that lays eggs, she
has a longer and slender abdomen and her reproductive
organs are fully developed.

The queen is confined to the hive until it is time for her
to mate. She then leaves the hive and unites in flight with
one or more males. From this one mating act she receives
enough sperm cells to fertilize the eggs she will lay during

her lifetime. Unlike the other members of the hive, the queen lives for several years. Egg-laying keeps her busy. Tirelessly, she may drop some fifteen hundred eggs into separate comb cells in a twenty-four-hour period. If she ever leaves the hive again, it is only because she is being replaced by a new young queen. When this happens the old queen, now an aged dowager, takes a swarm with her to a temporary home and finally to a place where a new colony is founded.

The males play a very limited part in the bee colony. They are plump, large-eyed and stingless, with brains smaller than those of the females. Those "successful" males who mate with the queen are immediately paralyzed, fall to earth and soon die. The remaining drones only live briefly beyond the time for mating. They are soon evicted from the hive. The outcasts starve, lacking the ability to procure their own food or to defend themselves.

The hive now becomes a totally female society, devoted entirely to raising the new generation. However, this is not, as is commonly suggested, "a matriarchal society." The queen does not really rule over anyone. There is neither tyranny nor oppression. In a bee colony, the members of both sexes have habitual roles which severely limit the range of their activity. For social bees, this is a way of living that has evolved through natural selection, a pattern that insures survival.

A bee colony does not leave mating to chance. Members of the two sexes are present in the hive, their roles clearly defined. The advantages of living together may go a long way toward explaining the social life not only of bees but of many other animal communities as well. By forming in groups, animals may very well insure their own success. Otherwise, the search for mates might be long and unsuccessful. A major hazard of life in the wild is the failure of animals to reproduce themselves. Often male and female of the same species must somehow find each other within the cold, dark depths of the sea, across the spacious wilderness of the Arctic or in the vast rain forests of the tropics.

In the bee colony, males and females are part of the same hive. Von Frisch showed that their sexual roles are distinct not only during the reproductive period but lifelong. Similar relationships are found in the societies of termites, ants and wasps.

Von Frisch's work, carried on persistently through the early decades of the twentieth century, made him more than a specialist in honeybees. In an era when both biology and psychology were developing a deep interest in animal behavior, the Austrian provided a model of scientific research and achievement.

In the winter of 1973, Karl von Frisch was awarded one of the highest honors known to the world of science. He and two others, Konrad Lorenz and Nikolaas Tinbergen, were presented with the Nobel Prize "for their discoveries concerning organization and elicitation of individual and social behavior patterns."

The three were hailed together as "the most eminent founders of a new science, the comparative study of behavior." However, they had each done their scientific work separately. They held, in fact, quite differing views on the question that has continued to confound the science of animal behavior — the matter of instinct.

4 · The Ceremonies of Birds

Tall and dense pines blocked out the sun as we wandered, lost, in the Bavarian woods. The clue that pressed us onward was a small signpost, M.P.I.V. My companion and I stumbled along a narrow logging road, its ruts and pocks flooded by the morning rains.

By late afternoon we found it — the "science village" that appeared on no map. This was the Max Planck Institut für Verhaltensphysiologie, a hidden-away segment of a great research institution that is headquartered in Munich. This branch of it was the nature laboratory of Konrad Lorenz.

From the wide publicity given Lorenz, the public has probably formed its most vivid picture of an animal behavior scientist. Genial, outspoken, colorful, Lorenz has appeared in striking news photos that showed him deep in the middle of a lake, up to his neck in waterfowl, or lost in the thoughtful study of a wasp nest as he tugged his beard tuft and puffed an unlighted pipe, or trailing a string of newly hatched goslings to whom he was "mother goose." He is one of this century's outstanding figures in animal research. For decades, he was driven tirelessly by what he considered the vastness of his own ignorance and the yawning gaps in scientific knowledge about animal behavior.

M.P.I.V. was his secluded place in southern Bavaria — a refuge for both wildlife and scientists. Members of a select research group gathered here in the early 1950s to work with Lorenz, one of the builders of the new science which he calls ethology.

Here the research team found Lorenz surrounded by wild greylag geese who had never learned to fear human beings. The waters of the lake abounded with species available for study in their native habitats. Lorenz' group of men and women lived among untamed, uncaged animals to whom they probably appeared as members of a strange outsize, flightless and harmless species. Among the frogs and salamanders, Lorenz, too, was a "two-lived" amphibian, moving between land and water. Around this small lake, in its reedy marshes and the encircling forests, he crowned a bright career in the study of how animals behave.

Since his earliest childhood, Konrad Lorenz was attracted to the study of nature. As a youngster in the Vienna

Woods, he had released a wild bird bought for four schillings in a pet shop. He got his money's worth from the sight of the jackdaw soaring to freedom.

That act of liberation was the beginning of a lifelong relationship between Lorenz and free-living creatures. He became an ethologist long before the study of animal behavior was an established science.

The winner of the Nobel Prize could, in 1973, recall the beginnings of his career, early periods of poverty and frustration. In his noisy, crowded home, he and his wife tried to live among assorted mice and monkeys, children and lemurs, geese and grandparents.

"How sad and mentally stunted is a caged monkey or parrot, and how incredibly alert, amusing and interesting is the same animal in complete freedom," Lorenz remarked. The research animals which had the run of his home were less than housebroken. His parrots nipped all the buttons from the garments on the family clothesline; the wild birds ate their fill from the berry bushes and later stained the furniture with bright purple spots; and the great geese that spent the night in the Lorenz bedroom left by the window before dawn with a whoosh of wings.

He recognized that he himself was a member of a strange breed. "Who else," he asked, "would dare to ask his wife to allow a tame rat to run free around the house, gnawing neat little circular pieces out of the sheets to furnish her nests in the Sunday hats?" And who but Lorenz would think of protecting his small child not by caging the roving animals, but by putting the baby into an enclosure?

He became convinced that work in a natural setting was the only way he could observe animals as they truly are. And while his research sites were not exactly virgin wilderness, he kept them as unspoiled as possible. Throughout his career, Lorenz' method has been to compare the behaviors of many species. He shunned only the domesticated and laboratory-raised and isolated animals. Instead, he studied free-living groups and pairs in their year-round and lifelong behaviors.

But he chose only certain species for special attention. He was interested least of all in the mammals, which are guided largely by their sense of smell. Fishes and birds are more like human beings, if only in their strong dependence on eyesight and visual communication. He specialized in geese and ducks — not the barnyard varieties but their wilder kin. And by watching them as they watched and responded to each other, Lorenz amassed a detailed record of their typical behaviors.

The animals at M.P.I.V. were free to come and go — and to vanish at times. These were not the rigorous study and testing conditions of the research laboratories, with their highly controlled artificial environments, their isolation cages, puzzle boxes, mazes and electronic monitors. But Lorenz was in search of natural behavior patterns.

Experiments were an important part of the work. But these were used to substantiate what had been repeatedly observed. Often the experiments consisted merely of making slight shifts in the natural environment in order to check animal responses. At times, such experimentation almost looked like the playing of idle pranks. But the purpose was serious.

A mother duck might suddenly find her nest filled with eggs in a wide range of colors, sizes and shapes; did she really know her own? Or a tape recorder might play a variety of artificial mating calls; what sounds really attracted the female to the male? Some studies were set up to find out whether an individual animal responds sexually to another individual — or does it simply react to a shape, a scent, a color, a set of sounds, a series of gestures? And how much does reproductive behavior depend on the time of the year, the food supply, temperature, light, safe nesting conditions?

As head of the M.P.I.V. research center, Lorenz directed

the work of a team of fellow scientists, assistants, students. Their fieldwork was often made difficult by the fact that wild animals are least likely to nest, mate or raise their young in places that are easy for researchers to find or reach or observe.

But the close study of animals holds perils even greater than sunburn, bee sting or exposure to storm and frost. Familiarity with the daily habits of wildlife can make one forget that they are animals. After weeks or months of study, they are no longer look-alikes. A wildfowl or a pond fish becomes a unique individual, acquires a personality, even a pet name.

The human researcher is then in some danger from a disability called "mirror vision" — seeing in animals something that appears to be "only human." It is all too easy to credit a duck with having a human mind instead of a bird brain, or to attribute human emotions to finch, frog or fish. And how misleading it can be to assume from their expressions that they are feeling remorse, courage, spitefulness, revenge or pity!

On one occasion, Lorenz and a group of students were looking at jewelfish, which habitually gather up their wandering young in their mouths in order to carry them back to the nest. A male was chewing on a large worm which was too big for a single swallow. Suddenly, a tiny, lost jewelfish offspring appeared, and the father scooped it into his mouth along with the remains of the worm. Lorenz and his students were aware of the fish's crisis — in his mouth at the same time were two substances which must somehow go two separate ways!

Lorenz described the drama: "For many seconds the father jewelfish remained riveted, and one could almost see how his feelings were working. Then he solved the conflict in a way for which one was bound to feel admiration. He spat out the whole contents of his mouth. Then the father turned resolutely to the worm and ate it up, without haste but all the time with one eye on the child. When he had finished eating, he inhaled the baby and carried it home to its mother." Lorenz' students, rapt in the whole tense scene, broke into hearty applause.

In an entirely new era of science, Lorenz appeared somewhat like the nineteenth-century naturalists. Like them, he too was adept at observation in natural habitats, with special talents for blending unseen into a spruce bog, waiting with incredible patience for the hatching of a clutch of fish eggs, or gaining acceptance at the nest site of herons. But unlike the woodland wayfarers of an earlier day, Lorenz brought to his research a highly scientific discipline and system — and most of all, the new insights of the century in biology that followed Darwin.

Charles Darwin had suggested new guidelines for the biologist. From a common and simple origin, animals had in millions of years developed an endless variety of bodily forms. In what ways did each structure help living beings to survive and reproduce? How did a particular shape of wing or color of fur or length of tongue better fit a species for life in its natural environment?

These were the kinds of Darwinian questions that Lorenz asked in his study of animal behavior. To him, the process of evolution clearly had shaped not only the bodies of animals but also the manner in which species mated or formed colonies or constructed nests or nurtured their young. Lorenz studied these behaviors as evolved adaptations to needs and habitats.

By watching the conduct of many types of closely related ducks, Lorenz was not only able to see what goes on in societies not ordinarily open to human beings; he was also privileged to see the workings of evolution. For each of these species had acquired its own special reproductive behaviors through the selection process. It was as though he was able to look backward through an immensity of

time, peering across uncounted centuries into the distant past, viewing the rise of animal generations and the development of new types of behavior which better fitted species for the conditions of their lives.

Did natural selection equip the male mallard duck with its green cap, the wood duck with its small body and long legs, the gadwall with its unusual bill, the pintail with its pointed hind end? Then the same life-serving processes of nature gave these same ducks the reproductive habit of piling leaves on top of a nestful of eggs; the practice of nesting in tree hollows; the mutual chin-raising ceremony of a mating gadwall pair; the distinctive "burp" of a pintail greeting.

Lorenz did not view himself as a specialist in the conduct of animal males and females toward each other. But out of the enormous volume of his studies emerged a detailed picture of the vital pairing process which leads to reproduction.

As he studied how the two sexes react toward each other, he witnessed an astonishing variety of male-female conduct. These behaviors were not random, haphazard, peculiar and unrelated acts. Instead, they seemed to appear and reappear in uniform ways and in orderly sequence. Much of what he saw was colorful displays, intricate movements and ceremonies of grace and beauty. Some of it reminded him of his own romantic courting days as a young man in Vienna. Lorenz has never been shy about giving descriptive human names to animal behavior. And what he saw being performed by fishes and birds he did not hestitate to call "courtship."

The animal in the wilderness lives in a state of unending danger. That is the main condition of its environment. The terrors of its world are countless and constant, the perils great, the death rate high.

It is against this harsh reality that the ethologist has looked at the behavior of wildlife. Much of what animals do appears to be a response to risk. Storm and drought, frost and famine are among the year-round killers. Predators and parasites are everywhere. Some of the hazards come from one's own kind, even perhaps from members of one's own group. And to expose one's self even once may be once too often.

Among the birds Lorenz studied there seemed to be full trust only between parent and offspring. They were close to each other bodily over long periods of brooding and nurturing. But no other bird relationship is quite so confident and sharing. Even the mating of male and female partners rarely begins with mutual trust.

In fact, what Lorenz saw was fierce hostility during the first approaches of pairs of wild geese who might later become mates for life. He focused his attention, and his field glasses, on this fascinating problem.

The birds that he saw coming together as mating pairs were at the outset fearful, cautious, hostile. They had first to identify each other as members of the same species as themselves. They also had to recognize each other as members of the opposite sex. And this is by no means a simple matter — even in those species where the two sexes differ in appearance. In some way it was necessary for these animals to communicate that they were available to each other as mates.

To Lorenz these pairing animals seemed torn by conflicting tendencies. Would they attack or mate or flee? As he saw them, they were faced with a double problem of survival. On the one hand they appeared to be protecting themselves against possible danger, wary against the unknown stranger. And yet the very future of their species was also at stake in Lorenz' view. For unless they overcame their fear and hostility, no sexual reproduction would ever take place.

From his places of concealment, Lorenz peered at wild greylag geese, intently studying their every movement. He was caught up in the scene, a spectator wondering how the processes of evolution had "solved" the life-and-death crisis of a species.

Suddenly, the pattern of behavior in the pairing geese took clear form. Typically, male and female had greeted each other with open animosity, making the threatening head and neck and body movements of geese preparing for battle. But now quickly the gander turned his attention to another male nearby. Toward this second male, the pairing gander unloosed a flurried sham attack, hissing, pecking, chasing. Having run off the second male, the gander returned to the female.

What Lorenz now witnessed he could only describe as a "triumph ceremony." Male and female joined in rolling and cackling together, calling to each other, stretching necks skyward side by side, uttering wild cries. To Lorenz, the performance expressed sheer joy in victory, as if a great battle had been fought and won. The partners sharing in this rite seemed strongly drawn together, as though "having something in common which has to be defended against outsiders."

They were now bonded in a way that ended the hostility between them and permitted nesting, mating, brooding, nurturing. "The bond that holds the goose pair together for life is the triumph ceremony and not the sexual relations between mates," Lorenz recorded. "It holds them together and enables them to stand together against a hostile world." He observed that, once joined, these pairs stayed together continuously, irrespective of whether they had young to protect or territory to defend or enemies to fight off. Again and again, the triumphant cry would be their greeting to each other, seeming to renew their unity against the dangers of their world.

To Lorenz, the wild geese seemed to be acting out the drama of Romeo and Juliet. The plot held conflict and uncertainty, fear and longing, aggression and affection. Male and female first met as both enemies and lovers, succeeding at last in overcoming the obstacles that held them apart.

Greylag pairing forms a bond that may last through a half-century of unity for a couple of these long-lived birds. Lorenz found their particular style of courting strikingly unusual. But then no two species pair in exactly the same way.

Pairing ceremonies are found in forms of life ranging from the insects to the higher mammals. The courtship performance varies in different species from very simple to elaborate, from brief to prolonged, from once-in-a-lifetime to a rite repeated every season. The behavior is communication between male and female by whatever senses they can best reach each other. Movement, color, sound, touch, smell and taste are used. Often the male begins the performance — but that is not the rule for every species. Males most often have special bodily features for sending out spectacular courting signals — but some females are not lacking in ways to display.

Wild turkeys pump up their scarlet wattles. Female baboons exhibit their bright-colored rumps. The peacock (the male peafowl) spreads his magnificent rainbow of tail feathers, clatters his quills, screams loudly, slowly turns and models himself before the drably colored peahen. The male tern offers the female a fish. The porcupine sprays his prospective mate with urine. The night heron performs his ungainly courting dance first on one foot and then on the other. Buffalo bulls stage contests of strength before female audiences. In the world of the herring gull, the female makes the opening gesture with a loud "kiloo." The male fighting fish builds a bubble nest and swims in tight circles around the female of his choice.

Lorenz observed the autumn bonding of wildfowl pairs which were not to mate until the following April. But early spring is more generally the season of courtship, when the wild world seems to stir and throb and blaze and resound with countless signals between male and female. Fireflies flash at each other in the night. But only bright sunlight spurs the courting display of sunfishes. Swamplands echo the shrill cries of male peepers and the throaty bass of large frogs. The varied howls of jackals, coyotes and wolves arise from the silence of lonely plains. The springtime world seems to be set into a rising beat by the click of male crickets rubbing their hard wing cases, the ardent songs of newly arrived migrant birds, the roar of alligators, the bellowings from the seal islands, the whine of mosquitoes on their courting flights. Woodpeckers drum in rapid tempo, cranes trumpet, cicadas rasp their wings, jackals cry out, and whippoorwills endlessly repeat their rhythmic calls.

Some pairing animals behave in ways that can only be described as dance or play. On the mid-American plain, prairie chickens assemble in a circle to watch the strutting, booming males perform a courtship quadrille. Butterflies forming partnerships tumble gracefully with each other in an aerial ballet. Many pairing fishes cavort about their nests. On warm beaches, the male fiddler crabs dance the females along in the crooks of their single enormous claw arms. Roused from hibernation, snakes begin their slow twining movements. In the woodlands, the courting dances of numerous small mammals take the form of a chase. On the ponds where they live, pairs of lobe-footed grebes perform their long-necked, dignified movements, matching each other in precision and symmetry.

In his detailed studies of mallard ducks, Lorenz showed how courting fits into the many phases of the year-round behavior of this species. Wild cousin of the barnyard duck, the mallard is a far-flying migrant. Although it lives at both ends of its migratory range and at points between, "home" is the place where it breeds.

Mallards migrate in flocks. And courtship begins within large mixed groups. But these groupings give way to the bonding of pairs. The drake is typically searching out suitable sites for a nest long before the female is ready for nesting, mating and egg-laying. The mallard male not only exhibits special behaviors in preparation for mating; he also undergoes a striking change of appearance. For por-

MALE PRAIRIE CHICKENS

FEMALE PRAIRIE CHICKENS

tions of the year, he is utterly dull in color, like the female of the species. But as the time for pairing approaches, the male acquires a headdress of shimmering green feathers, a white collar, bright red or purple flecks on the breast, gray markings on the flanks and black tail covers which curl upward. Showy, resplendent, gaudy, he flaunts all of his finery in a jaunty display. To each series of perky movements by the male, the female responds with her own.

These wild waterfowl do their courting mainly on the surfaces of freshwater ponds, slow streams and marshes. Lorenz has minutely recorded their complementary pairing behaviors, giving each a descriptive name. "Grunt whistle," "nod-swimming," "body-shaking," "head-up-tail-up" were among the sounds and movements he detailed.

Each of these displays was carried out according to an orderly pattern, typical and unique for the members of this species. In this way, pairing was accomplished, leading to mating. The various behaviors seemed to serve in "bringing together members of the right species, of the right sexes, in the right place at the right time for reproduction."

Descriptions of the many varieties of animal courtship are among the most wonder-filled studies of ethologists. But courting is only the beginning of the process of reproduction, and that is its real significance in animal life. Scientific experimentation has yielded the important fact that numerous species cannot produce offspring without courtship.

In spite of Lorenz' exploratory work, the pair-bonding of animals is still a realm of mystery. Much research remains to be done, and every discovery reveals new problems. Modern research has found flaws in earlier findings about how and why pairing behaviors occur. Even Lorenz has not escaped the searching questionings of his fellow scientists.

*

In the unknowing wilderness of a new science — ethology — Konrad Lorenz appeared as a strange bird, making strong claims, challenging accepted ideas with bold new ones. He became fair game for many-sided criticism. In the last two decades, Lorenz has had as many opponents as defenders. Few of his critics could match him in field research. No one dared to question the accuracy of his scientific observations. But he has drawn heavy fire.

It was charged that through his use of misleading language, animals were made to appear as though they were human; that he overstressed the "innate" in explaining the basis for the activities of higher animals; that he made broad interpretations of his data which were sometimes in error when applied to individual cases; that he relied on his animal research to draw sweeping conclusions about human behavior.

Crusty and keen-witted, Lorenz fought off the faultfinders. But by the early 1970s, Lorenz was forced to give way on many points. The rapidly expanding research on animals was producing important new information. All of the sciences probing the processes of life were added to the understanding of the way animals function. And Lorenz well realized that all the final answers could not be discovered by one man with a pair of field glasses standing at the side of a wild pond.

A Nobel Prize climaxed his successful career. But not even Lorenz believes that everything he had concluded was correct or valuable. No true scientist tackles new fields of research and publishes his findings without risking error and criticism.

Fellow scientists have pointed out that Lorenz' enduring place in ethology is secure — "if only he didn't confuse animals with people." His 1963 book, *On Aggression,* became a widely acclaimed best-seller. But it was also sharply criticized for drawing false analogies between the self-protection behaviors of animals and the destructive, warlike conduct of human societies.

Perhaps he was strongly influenced by early years in Europe's most romantic city — but the Vienna-born Lorenz has been chided for his fanciful reports which picture fishes as "completely transformed by love," and wildfowl as smitten by "love at first sight." He has also opened himself to the accusation of bringing to his scientific studies the prejudices of a male brought up in a male-dominated society, too ready to see all females as inferior.

This was his description of a pair of jackdaws: "It is really touching to see how affectionate these two wild creatures are with each other. Every delicacy that the male finds is given to his bride and she accepts it with the plaintive begging gestures and notes otherwise typical of baby birds."

"Sentimental rubbish!" has been the response of many scientists to such accounts of animal wooing.

Lorenz has hotly defended his viewpoint. "You think I humanize the animal?" he has written. "Perhaps you do not know that what we are wont to call 'human weakness' is, in reality, nearly always a pre-human factor and one which we have in common with the higher animals? Believe me, I am not mistakenly assigning human properties to animals; on the contrary, I am showing you what an enormous animal inheritance remains in man, to this day."

The rage of controversy around Lorenz takes nothing away from his valuable scientific achievements. These, including his work on pairing and courtship, are key pieces set into the vast, unfinished puzzle of animal behavior.

5 · Pairs and Parents

That males and females do not always behave "as they should" is a finding often made by a scientist investigating some species other than his own.

Niko Tinbergen was amused by just such a discovery in the summer of 1933. This student of wildlife, far from the shores of his native Holland, was winding up a venturesome year in Greenland as zoologist with a small Dutch scientific expedition. Tinbergen was still in his twenties when he set sail aboard the four-master *Gertrud Rask*. He took his bride with him on what could hardly be called a honeymoon.

For an eager and curious naturalist, the year in the Arctic was full of revelation and wonder. The wildlife he observed there was familiar enough in form. But the behaviors of some of these species, seen at close range, were sometimes beyond belief.

Tinbergen must have felt at moments like young Charles Darwin who, a hundred years before, had embarked on a similar scientific journey. Darwin's memorable round-the-world "Voyage of the *Beagle*" was to introduce him to strange varieties of animals and to open his eyes to the process of evolution. His observations led the British biologist slowly to the realization that "any being, if it vary however slightly in any manner profitable to itself . . . will have a better chance of surviving, and thus be naturally selected."

Tinbergen observed Arctic birds, fishes and mammals with one main question in mind: In what ways were their peculiar behaviors "profitable," improving their chances for survival and reproduction? None behaved more oddly than did a long-distance migrant, the red-necked phalarope.

Early one June morning, Tinbergen spotted the first of these shorebirds to reach the east Greenland coast. In migratory species, an advance "scouting" group is ordinarily made up entirely of males. The early arrivals of these phalaropes were all females.

From that moment on, the flocks of these small wading birds continued to reveal one astonishing trait after another. In contrast to the color patterns found in other species, female phalaropes were much more brilliantly hued than the males, yellow-striped with rust collars and striking markings in gray, white and black. It was not the males but the females who were the singers, uttering loud, hoarse, rhythmic calls.

Tinbergen now watched the females in courting displays, flying and swimming in a fashion which attracted

the males. The she-phalaropes proved to be vigorous
fighters, fiercely attacking other members of the same sex.
They also showed aggressive, blustering behavior toward
males but never carried out their threats.

As the summer days and weeks passed, the phalaropes
were paired and mated. Females were now taking the lead
in nesting activities at the pond sides. The couples joined
in making "scrapes," a number of shallow digs in the sand.
These sites were periodically revisited by the pairs of
partners. The time had come for egg-laying.

Fascinated, Tinbergen gave his full attention to one pair
of phalaropes. As he focused on these mates, the female
suddenly burst into song and flew off, with the male following close behind. The pair, led by the female, made a
tour of all their scrapes. In the fourth one they visited, the
female laid an egg while her mate looked on. During the
next two days, both Tinbergen and the male bird kept vigil
as the second and third eggs were laid.

It was soon clear that the ceremony of showing the male
the chosen nesting place was a matter of vital importance.
The female departed as soon as the eggs were laid! And the
task of brooding the eggs and nurturing the chicks was left
entirely to the male. "Obviously," wrote Tinbergen, "the
'nest-showing' ceremony was the means by which the
female made the male follow her to where she would lay
the eggs, so that he could learn their whereabouts."

Tinbergen sat up late in the Arctic summer nights recording in his notebook bird behavior such as he had never
seen before. He had learned from the phalarope: You can't
ever be sure from observing animal behavior which sex is
which!

The red-necked phalarope was only one of the species
made famous by Tinbergen's detailed scientific reports on
their conduct. After the Greenland expedition, the next
forty years led Niko (short for Nikolaas) Tinbergen "brows-

MALE PHALAROPE NESTING

ing in a variety of habitats." He remained a stalker of animals in their wild haunts — the wilder the better.

Digger wasps, sticklebacks, newts, owls, water beetles and gulls attracted his intense interest. Tinbergen was also increasingly in demand as teacher, filmmaker, writer, animal photographer, TV lecturer. Migrant and energetic in his research, Tinbergen carried his work to every continent in all seasons. He settled at last at Oxford University in England, but only on the promise that he could be free-ranging at will.

It has been hard to keep him in the classroom and the laboratory. He has sometimes appeared there in hiking boots and knapsack, ready to move on, a slender, spectacled outdoorsman with steely gray hair and a year-round suntan. His field equipment is usually simple — field glasses, a notebook and an old chair, along with plenty of curiosity and patience.

His conversation about his work, rich in personal anecdotes, is modest and thoughtful. He can often be heard saying, "I don't know," and, "I was wrong" — two phrases that are in keeping with the difficulties of developing a new science. But Tinbergen is recognized as one of the people who have made ethology one of the really important special fields of modern biology.

In the awarding of the 1973 Nobel Prize, which he shared with Konrad Lorenz and Karl von Frisch, Tinbergen was cited for his "ingenious experiments." He has operated by a few guiding principles. He carefully balances field and laboratory work in the firm belief that "we should continue to observe and describe before we experiment."

He views animals' habits as their adaptation to an environment. Observing behavior, he asks, "Of what use is it?" The question does not often have an easy answer, but the query is always intriguing to him.

Tinbergen has rarely been tempted to equate the behaviors of lower animals with those of human beings. If Lorenz brought to light the ways in which animals pair, Tinbergen has clearly described reproductive behavior, revolving around the animal's home base, the nest site, the territory. But Tinbergen has never tried to fit males and females into fixed roles as "nestbuilders," "breadwinners," "homemakers," and the rest. The phalarope was only one of the many species he studied that violated popular notions of how the two sexes should behave.

Tinbergen is always amused at the responses of some of his male friends when he tells them about females he has known — in the wilderness. "It is a very shocking fact to most of my friends when I mention it to them," he says, "that the initiative in lovemaking is usually taken by the female — in the world of the herring gull."

Since early boyhood, Niko Tinbergen has been under the spell of the herring gulls. He remembered them as the last "blizzard" of the winter season.

On a day in late March, the sky would suddenly fill with what appeared as enormous snowflakes swirling to earth. The gulls had returned to the Dutch shores of the North Sea. Pearl white and elegant, they glided to and fro, glowing in the sun. In a moment the mass descent was over. Suddenly the storm of wings ended and the gulls were spread out over the beach, standing in pairs.

Long years later, Tinbergen returned to these birds for study. His year of the herring gull was 1936, when he was professor of zoology at Leyden University, with the gulleries only an hour's bicycle ride away. Tinbergen and his students steeped themselves in the full range of wild gull lore. He was now an expert in the fine art of bird-watching. Let's watch him at work.

A small tent suddenly appears near a nest of brooding gulls. Nervous at first, the nesting mates soon get used to the strange structure. Every day or two, the tent moves closer and closer to the birds. Tinbergen is now in effective spying range, two meters from the nest. Each morning, he and a friend enter the tent as quietly as possible. And when the gulls see the friend leave, they begin to behave as though all strangers have vanished. Inside the tent, Tinbergen settles down with coffee jug, sandwiches, note pad and sketch pad, his binoculars fixed on the nest through a small masked window. So begins a ten-hour watch of the intimate behavior of a gull pair.

Tinbergen is not bored. These long periods of what he calls "watching and wondering" are his time for thinking about the meaning of what he sees. He observes and records and mulls every gesture, outcry, activity of the gull pair and of the other animals about them.

Each wild bird has been banded for identification with colored rings. The journal records the day's events in precise detail: "15th May, 1936. 6:13 a.m. Male 4 is on station, ten birds on club not far away. Some birds begin to utter the mew call and the trumpeting call. Male 4 promptly attacks the trumpeting birds."

Herring gulls live in two habitats. They winter in areas where there is plenty of food matter washed ashore and strewn on the beach. However, the summer breeding sites are more isolated, safer from predators. In their winter flocks, the gulls live as single individuals. But they come to the breeding grounds either as previously formed pairs or as seekers of partners. Those still unpaired stay in a large group which Tinbergen has called "the club."

Once mated, male and female stay close together throughout the breeding season. Old pairs return to the same territory year after year, perhaps throughout life. They breed where they have successfully bred before, and sometimes in the very places where they were born.

Tinbergen's reports emphasized that paired herring gulls are closely attached to each other and to their home. Male and female choose the site together and share the work of nest-building. When the eggs are laid they take turns in brooding them, relieving each other on the nest every few hours. While either eggs or chicks are present, the home is never unguarded. And both male and female join in defending a territory of a few square meters.

For herring gulls, a territory is important mainly because it affords protection for the young against predators, Tinbergen concluded. His studies of many species have shown, however, that territories have a variety of uses — or none at all. He has helped to clear up a phase of animal behavior clouded by much misunderstanding.

Some writers have tried to suggest that the claiming of territory shows that not only animals but also human beings have a natural "land hunger," a driving need to own property. In reality, territorial behavior is largely limited to most species of birds and some of mammals. Territories are rare among insects and also among other land and water species without backbones. Among the vertebrates, reptiles, amphibians, and schooling fishes seldom claim territories.

A territory, Tinbergen has shown, is most often an area used only seasonally for carrying out certain specific biological functions — mainly those linked with reproduction. It is a place where courtship, mating and nesting may take place. Sometimes it offers safety or food for the young. Rarely is a territory defended throughout the year. In most cases, it is temporarily held, and the occupants have no interest in it once that brief period is over. In a variety of ways, breeding animals outline the boundaries of their claims and signal "Keep out!" to members of their own species. But other animals are free to come and go, and the territorial boundaries of many species ordinarily crisscross and overlap each other.

Recent studies show that territorial habits may vary with food supplies. In those years or seasons when food is either scarce or very abundant, many species form colonies instead of defending territories as mating pairs. If roving hunter species claim territories at all, these are changed constantly. Often male mammals claim not a plot of ground but an area surrounding a desired female. Turtles, which bury their eggs deeply and safely, show no interest in territories.

In his study of the territorial herring gull, Tinbergen revealed that both eggs and chicks are highly vulnerable to raiders, even though they are colored so as to be hardly visible and nests are also camouflaged. In this species, the scientist pointed out, territories serve to space out the nests, and as a result, predators are less likely to wreak damage on a large number of herring gull offspring at once.

In many of the species investigated by Tinbergen, defense against predators is fierce and often carried on by both males and females. However, fighting between members of the same species is usually more bluff than battle. From the onset of the mating season, the peaceful relations within an animal group are shattered by rivalry. Most often it is the males who flaunt their brute strength and ferocity. The male display often serves a double purpose — attracting females and threatening other males.

The fiddler crab waves aloft its one enormous claw. A male gorilla beats its drumlike chest. The screech owl puffs itself and spreads its feathers so as to appear double in size. And the horned toad becomes very prickly. The typical masculine fashion among fishes is to spread their gill covers; various male birds raise their crests and expose their most brightly colored parts; many mammals bare their teeth. During the mating season, the wilderness resounds with male roaring, snorting, screeching, hoofstamping.

It is a "war of nerves" in which one rival or the other commonly surrenders long before there is any bloodshed. Rarely does any deadly violence take place over mates or territory. Commonly, the sham battle is won by the animal that can assume the most threatening posture, brandish the fiercest weapons, make the loudest noises or unloose the most offensive smells.

The most familiar wooing and claiming behavior is birdsong. Human beings may consider many of the songs as musical performances of great beauty. But they are signals to which other birds of the same species respond. To the ethologist, a birdcall may reveal many things: the identity of the bird and its sex; the extent of its territory; the condition or location of its nest; its readiness for mating; a state of alarm or fear; a warning to other birds; or a signal to its offspring or to the flock.

Among wildlife, so many natural events "are determined by their usefulness." This has been Niko Tinbergen's main guide to understanding the animal behaviors that often appear at first to be so puzzling.

He has discovered the secrets in many a bird's song, unraveled mysteries of behavior in animal tracks, and learned the landmarks by which a digger wasp is able to find its own home buried deep in a sand dune. Tinbergen spent painstaking months of research learning why a black-headed gull quickly rids its nest of the eggshell once a chick has hatched, studying exactly how the shells attract predators. Some of his most remarkable research has shown, as in the case of the phalarope, that nature does not adhere to rigid patterns of male and female behavior.

"Even the most improbable things an animal does," he has written, "can be seen to meet what the natural environment demands."

He has disclosed for us why a fish called the stickleback fans its nest with its fins.

In the tank, the puny little fish stood on its head, fierce and pugnacious. The observer, who knew all the signs of a stickleback "itching for a fight," could hardly hold back his laughter. The fish's "enemy" was its own image, seen in a mirror.

To Niko Tinbergen, the experiment clearly revealed how aggressive behavior is linked to the mating season. At another time of year, the male stickleback would not react in this way toward its own image in the mirror, nor toward any other male. But the small fish in the tank had begun its reproductive cycle, as indicated by the red spot on its belly. And the appearance of any other red-marked stickleback brought on warlike behavior.

In fact, the image of the male rival need hardly be very

realistic in order for this testy little fish to get its dander up. A cardboard model with a red underside would do just as well.

One spring day, Tinbergen was in his laboratory in Leyden where a number of tanks containing sticklebacks were lined up along the windows. At that moment, a red mail truck passed by in the street outside. Tinbergen described what happened. "All the male sticklebacks dashed to the window as far as their tanks allowed them and 'attacked' the red mail van as it passed a hundred yards from the lab, responding to it as they would to a rival male, which is itself red."

The three-spined stickleback is one of the species that has reached world fame through Tinbergen's experiments. It is a gray green, finger-length fish covered with spiny fins, tough skin and bony armor that make it a poor meal for larger fishes. Its natural haunts are ponds and streams.

To Tinbergen, its peculiar behavior was not just a curiosity. He found in its habits a number of special adaptations to its environment. And he spent years observing and recording the activities of males and females. As a result, the private life story of the stickleback is better known than that of any other fish.

Throughout most of the year, sticklebacks move about in schools, brash, fearless and ravenous. As the male's belly becomes tinged with red, he quits the school and begins a chain of early summer behaviors that make him a remarkable mate and parent. While still unattached to any female, he undertakes alone to build a nest, digging in the sand, constructing a short tunnellike structure made of bits of reed and fiber held together with a gluey substance from his kidneys.

He is now in the center of a territory which he defends savagely against all other males of his kind. Experiments have shown that the closer he is to his nest the more violently he reacts to intruding rivals, with teeth bared and spines bristling. But should the stranger linger instead of fleeing, the stickleback often continues his scare tactics without carrying out the threat.

As mating time nears, his appearance becomes spectacular. His eyes shine brilliantly against the strong background colors, the scarlet belly and silver blue back. As egg-swollen females appear, he does an odd zigzag dance that seems to be both frightening and attractive to possible mates. At length, one of the females follows him toward the nest and he guides her into it.

Spawning occurs after the male has nudged the pregnant

female repeatedly with his snout. He enters the nest and fertilizes the eggs. The male now loses all further interest in this partner. She is driven from the nest.

"This is the end of the whole mating ceremony," Tinbergen reports. "There is no 'marriage,' no personal relationships and the female's whole task in reproduction is just to provide the eggs. The whole care of eggs and young is the male's job."

In the next few days, the male may bring several additional mates to the nest to lay eggs. But no females remain on the scene. In fact, while the male stickleback is caring for the eggs he zealously chases away any intruders, male or female.

For three weeks, until the young are hatched and grown, the male tends the nest with unfailing vigilance. In the closing acts of the reproductive cycle, he keeps the young together, sometimes scooping up the straying ones in his mouth, guarding them until they are old enough to go their own ways. Meanwhile, the male has been steadily fading in color, also losing his interest in defending the territory. Finally he returns to single life within the cooperative and leaderless school of sticklebacks, moving with them throughout the autumn and winter.

In stickleback behavior patterns, Tinbergen believed he saw the longtime workings of natural selection whereby every wild species acquires habits that are vitally useful. Bodily structures and ways of living are tested in living environments, and only those individuals favorably adapted continue to survive. Successful behavior patterns that are "adaptive" are handed down from one generation to the next through the genes. The stickleback proved to be a showcase of adaptive behaviors.

While the stickleback female was in the nest, the nudging movement made by the male against the base of the female's tail induced spawning. Up to this point, mating had proceeded by means of a number of visual stimuli;

now a touch stimulus was necessary. Tinbergen showed that the desired result could also be achieved by a human experimenter using a glass rod as a prod. He proved further that without the nudging the female could not spawn.

Equally dramatic were the activities of the male stickleback while the eggs were in the nest. The fish's movements consisted mainly of waving his fins constantly near the nest. While this behavior appeared strange at first to Tinbergen and his associates, they soon learned why the fanning was necessary. By this means, the eggs were ventilated, constantly supplied with fesh water and oxygen. Further experiments showed that without fanning the eggs would die.

Tinbergen took the view that adaptive behaviors are not simply those dictated by the needs of each single organism. "While many behavior elements are directly advantageous to the individual," he said, "there are other elements that are of no direct benefit to the individual but are of advantage to a group of individuals."

Behaviors may in fact be hazardous to the single organism, Tinbergen pointed out, but they are adaptive because they serve the mating pair, the offspring, the colony or the species as a whole. "Fighting, although in some respects a disadvantage to the individual," Tinbergen wrote, "is of great use to the species because it effects spacing out and thus tends to prevent harmful overcrowding."

In recent years, this distinguished scientist and his associates have dealt with a number of unanswered questions: What kinds of stimuli elicit various acts or chains of conduct? How much is behavior influenced by climate or season, the length of the day or the warmth of the sun? Do animals most often respond to "sign stimuli" received from other animals? Or are behaviors set into motion mainly "from within?"

Fortunately for the complex new science of animal behavior, its seekers are many and varied. When the trail of facts reaches a dead end in the wilderness, it often can be pursued further in the laboratory. The patient observer with the field glasses records as much as he can see; a further view may be visible to the prober with the microscope.

6 · The Wooing of Doves

The dove in the cage was ripe for egg-laying. But the experiment called for keeping this female alone and apart from any of its kind. While the experimenters waited patiently, not a single egg appeared.

Then came part two of the experiment. In another cage, behind a glass plate, a male dove was put on display. The male bowed and cooed. Almost at once, the female laid the first of her eggs.

Was this merely a simple automatic response to a visual stimulus? Or was there something deeper to be learned from this act of a female dove laying eggs at the mere sight of a male?

Daniel S. Lehrman, director of the Institute of Animal Behavior at Rutgers University in New Jersey, was intrigued by the fact that a chain of acts may often be set into motion by unseen factors, by something "more than meets the eye." In the case of the egg-laying dove, he discovered that she would not respond to just any male — only to one that produced all the cooing sounds and strutting postures of courtship display.

Lehrman began his career in biology as a city boy who sometimes skipped school in order to watch the warbler migrations, spring and fall, through New York's Central Park. He was an avid field naturalist who found himself deeply involved in experimental work.

For twenty years, until his death in 1972, Lehrman devoted himself faithfully to one species, the ring dove. He had previously ranged widely in working with many types of animals. But these studies only sent him finally homing toward the small doves whose cages filled his laboratory. He was a sturdy and sober-minded man, huge in bulk, but with a surgeon's delicate skills in his strong hands.

Lehrman stayed close to his laboratory and his caged birds, and he was happiest there. But he found himself in the center of the stormy controversy that continues to rage around the young science of animal behavior. Many of the scientists were drawn toward one of two opposing sides. Lehrman became the spokesman for one viewpoint, Konrad Lorenz for the other. The issues were vigorously debated, mainly in scientific journals and on university lecture platforms. This was a battle fought long-distance, across the sea, for the adversaries were mainly arrayed on the two sides of the Atlantic.

Lehrman was part of a large group of animal behavior researchers whose background lies mainly in the field of psychology. By contrast, the European ethologists have their roots in biology. The two groups developed conflicting methods, concepts, scientific goals.

The Europeans, under the guidance of Lorenz, tended to divide animal habits into two distinct types — learned behavior and unlearned. The Lehrman group, centered in America, saw little value in these either-or categories, preferring instead to concentrate on how behavior develops in the life of the individual, the pair, the group, the species.

Because of their interest in what is innate, inbred and instinctual, the Europeans were looking mainly for typical, "natural," uniform patterns of conduct. By contrast, the Americans were mainly concerned with variations from such patterns, as clues to discovering how certain types of stimuli affect behavior.

As Lehrman pointed out at the height of the debate, his experiments were aimed mainly at "producing effects through a variety of treatments" so as to learn how behavior develops. Lorenz, and those who followed him, steadfastly continued to work in the field, recording the common behaviors of wild species. They insisted that only such observations could reveal the workings of natural selection.

By the late 1960s the two opposing groups were in strong, open disagreement. Each criticized the other's scientific methods. The European ethologists were told that much of their field research was conducted without proper controls and that their conclusions lacked sufficient proof.

The Americans were informed that the artificial conditions in their laboratories could only produce artificial behavior. Their critics scoffed at animal research limited mainly to two domesticated species, the pigeon and the white rat.

The controversy has never been completely put to rest, but gradually it has subsided. Scientists on both sides, who have all contributed valuable work to this growing science, have begun to listen to each other more carefully, some-times finding out that what seemed to be differences in ideas were merely misunderstandings in language. By the mid-1970s tempers had cooled and the continuing debates have taken on a more friendly and reasoned tone.

Each side has learned from the criticisms of the other. For one thing, the experimental psychologists have begun to use a much broader range of animal species, widening their scope of study. Many of the European ethologists have backed away from their rigid views on instinct. Both sides have benefitted from the work of those scientists who were busy probing more deeply into the bodily changes in the tissues, organs and internal chemistry of animals en-gaged in various kinds of behavior.

New facts have come to light about the ability of animals to react in orderly ways to new stimuli. Experimentation has revealed that even such lowly creatures as flatworms can acquire changed behavior patterns through exposure to such stimuli as light flashes and electric shocks.

Research on many types of lower animals has revealed unsuspected learning abilities. The techniques of "be-haviorism" are aimed at teaching animals to perform by repeatedly rewarding apt behavior. The mouse can find its way through a complex maze to food or water or a mouse mate. An animal may perform simply in anticipation of being fondled. Another may do amazing deeds for another kind of reward — to be left in peace! Sometimes lab specimens can also learn without being bribed at all.

To say that an organism learns is not to suggest that there is a human mind inside the body of an animal. Creative intelligence, imagination, foresight, human understanding are not within the power of lower animals. The bee does not help build the hive out of a sense of family loyalty. A fox does not bury food because it remembers the winter past or foresees the winter ahead. And gulls do not construct nests because they anticipate laying eggs. Such animals do have abilities needed to perform these behaviors. And research shows that under certain conditions, with the proper stimuli, they will carry out certain acts that are typical for their species. But such behavior patterns may be modified.

New studies revealed that some types of outside stimuli may have an important effect on behaviors previously thought to be entirely innate. Experimenters proved that animals may begin responding to external stimuli even before they are born. A study of unhatched ducklings showed that they not only heard sounds but reacted to them with a faster heartbeat and responding sounds of their own. Another prober listened carefully and heard quail embryos calling to each other softly from inside their shells — an experience that may in some way influence their behavior patterns. Experiments with rats revealed that when pregnant mothers are placed under stress, this has an effect on the later behavior of their infants.

Research also disclosed that in the period immediately after birth, an animal acquires an amazing quantity of information about the world it has entered. Lorenz had himself become widely known for his experiments in which infant wildfowl became attached to him shortly after birth and remained "imprinted" by him. Since he was the first object that attracted their attention when they opened their eyes, these nestlings adopted him as their "mother." Lorenz used this experiment to stress the importance of instinctual behavior patterns. However, imprinting has since been recognized as a type of learning.

Many scientists have rejected the notion that behavior is like a set of recorded messages, each turned on by the proper switch. Nor do they liken an organism to a filling bowl from which behavior overflows whenever a certain level is reached. And serious doubts have been raised about Lorenz' suggestion of a lock-and-key mechanism, in which the proper stimulus opens a "door," thereby automatically releasing a sequence of unchangeable acts. Unlike the fixed operation of machines, the complex behavior of living things can rarely be explained in terms of a single cause or a simple device.

The "great dispute" among students of animal behavior probably came about largely because different groups of them had plucked separate bits and pieces of information out of the immense unknown. But the angry voices of discord died down as investigators became more awed by the vastness of their task and more aware of the need to approach it from multiple viewpoints in order to see the varied factors at work.

In the old fable, six blindfolded men could not separately discern the true form of an elephant. How much less could any one narrow and limited outlook explain how an elephant behaves?

Seek out the exact moment when animal mating begins — and what do you find? Is the action triggered by some deep and mysterious parental urge? Is it sparked by the coming together of male and female?

In reality, much reproductive behavior begins with the change in the length of the day. Most animals respond to the springtime increase in the hours of light. This tendency is probably an inherited one, a behavior that has proven to have a reproductive advantage. Animals that have acquired the habit of mating in the spring are usually assured of better conditions for raising their young, including a more abundant food supply.

Such favorable circumstances regulate the mating season for most species in the temperate zones of the earth. There are other factors controlling the breeding rhythms of animals in the Arctic regions, where day and night may be as much as six months long, or in the equatorial belt, where the daily duration of light and darkness hardly varies from one season to the next.

In his laboratory Daniel S. Lehrman produced day and night, spring and autumn at will. By regulating lights, temperature and humidity he set animals into untimely behaviors. He could in fact turn any season into the mating season. Moreover, he was able to vary mating behavior through making slight changes in environmental conditions. He showed that although animals may have strong tendencies to repeat certain typical behavior patterns, they are not limited to actions fixed by "blind instinct." Living things are affected in special ways by circumstances outside themselves. Light, food, weather have their effects on patterns of behavior. Even the lowliest animals seem able to respond to the daily conditions of their environment.

True, behavior is affected by an animal's genetic inheritance. Every species has its own behavioral tendencies. Animals of a certain kind may act in typical ways — unless other influences change their conduct.

Characteristic acts often make the members of a species appear as though they were all identical, spring-wound toy animals produced in the same factory. The mother bird stuffs food into the gaping maws of her fledglings. Spiders of a certain kind build webs that are almost exact copies of each other. Green turtles swim hundreds of miles to gather on a tiny ocean island they have never seen, the breeding ground of their species. A muskrat builds a particular type of den. The tree toad utters a unique call. A redwing blackbird is generally seen in a familiar marshy setting among reeds and cattails.

Sometimes animals will persist in characteristic acts even when they seem to accomplish nothing, or when the conditions which prompted the behavior have been changed. In a fight between two male antelopes, one of them lost his horns, but he was observed to continue the ritual fighting, posturing exactly the same way he would if the horns were still on his head. One scientist has described a starling going through the motions of catching

and eating a fly which should have been there, but wasn't. Gulls have persisted in sitting on their nests long after their eggs were removed and a set of painted cubes substituted for them.

At Rutgers, Lehrman put a ring dove pair into a cage which contained a ready-made nest and a clutch of dove eggs. The birds ignored the egg-and-nest gift, went ahead with their own courting behavior and built a second nest on top of the one they were given.

An experimenter who kept "stealing" one egg each day from a flicker's nest induced the bird to keep replacing the missing one. And over a period of months, the flicker laid an additional seventy-one eggs!

Animals do inherit the capability for behaving in certain ways. And it may often appear that nothing in the world can prevent them from carrying out acts they seem born and bound to perform. But Lehrman and a good many other experimental psychologists have shown how the most inbred behavior patterns may be modified by the animal's own experience.

Researchers studying birds have put them through an unbelievable range of unusual conditions that reveal how responsive they are to outside influences. Studies have shown animals acting in unpredicted ways.

The brooding of newborn may appear as a rather fixed kind of behavior — but changed temperature may determine how long a mother goose will sit on her nestlings. The song of a bird is not like the playback of a tape. Its call may be as changeable as the weather, as uncertain as the food supply, as variable as the stimuli from other birds. In one tropical region where the birds normally breed during the rainy spring season, an unusual spell of wet weather in autumn can stir the birds to mating behavior.

The number of eggs laid by certain birds seldom varies and birth rates usually conform to regular patterns. But studies have shown that when bird populations get too high, or the food supply too low, the number of eggs in a clutch may decline. A survey of an English species of titmice revealed that they breed in accordance with the current supply of caterpillars on which they feed.

An animal's behavior is generally influenced by that of other animals. They may respond to predators or prey. Most often, animals are stimulated by members of their own species — one of the same sex, or of the opposite sex, or the young. In most cases, the individual also reacts to the group of which it is a part.

Are these forms of "learned behavior"? Unfortunately,

this term has a variety of meanings and uses. The most common understanding of learning is that it is a process in which repeated experiences have a long-range effect on behavior. However, some scientists in this field define "learning" in a broad way. They may consider that any behavior prompted by an experience or by some changed condition in the environment is a kind of short-term learning.

Experimenters have become doubtful that there are any behavior patterns that cannot be varied by experience or learning. In the so-called isolation experiment animals are separated at birth from their parents and all other animals. They may be hatched from eggs in private incubators. As they grow in isolation, their behaviors are compared for similarities with those of other animals of their kind, perhaps those of sisters and brothers living more normal lives. However, scientists are not satisfied that it is possible to disentangle the purely innate from all other influences.

They have found that while the simpler forms of life are restricted in their learning, those on advanced levels of evolution tend to be more flexible in their conduct. Behavior patterns of the higher species are more likely to be influenced by lifetime experiences. Human beings are ruled least of all by the tyranny of what is inborn. Unlike protozoa, people are not locked into behavior stereotypes, the dull, standardized repetition of the typical conduct of others of their kind. Many birds and fish, mammals, and particularly primates, also have remarkable abilities to learn.

They learn through effort and reward, as does the shorebird that manages to open a clam shell. Or through imitation, as in the case of the chaffinch that fully develops its song only if it can hear the songs of other birds of its kind. They learn from experience, as does the bear cub that tries to tackle a skunk. Or by the trial-and-error method of a mouse in a maze. Or by practice, as with birds whose fledgling flights are wobbly and unsure.

Experiences crowded into the first hours, days, weeks of an animal's infancy often mold the behavior patterns of a lifetime. Lehrman and his associates have also shown that practice plays an important part in the ways that animals carry out later breeding behaviors. In numerous experiments, he revealed that males and females had clearly learned a great deal from their earlier experiences in nesting, mating, hatching eggs and brooding offspring. Research with primates has shown that only by practicing certain sexual behaviors through play does the young monkey or ape become an adult able to reproduce.

Animals sometimes learn slowly and with difficulty. But the ability to learn carries great advantages. The animal severely limited by inbred restraints on its behavior is helpless in dealing with new and unfamiliar situations. Whole species have disappeared because they were unable to learn how to deal with changing environments. However, every species alive today is a "success" because it has undoubtedly met the challenges of change and modified its behavior accordingly.

Living things inherit not the behaviors of their parents but the abilities to perform in certain ways. A striking example is the case of the female honeybees, the so-called workers, who build and guard and clean the hive, provide it with food and do everything except mating. The busy workers inherit these capabilities from the queen bee and a male — a pair of parents who do none of these things!

Animals do inherit what Lehrman called "guidelines" — a kind of framework which sets outer limits on the kinds of behavior of which they are capable. Their actual lifetime behaviors take place within this frame. In the case of the lowest animals, the frame is very narrow. Going up the evolutionary scale, the frame expands in scope, allowing for greater and greater freedom in the types of conduct that are possible.

While every offspring is limited in the range of its behaviors by the capabilities with which it is endowed at birth, it has potentials which it may or may not use. Its development depends on many factors outside itself — but also within.

Ring doves are small, hardy relatives of the common pigeon who seem to lose none of their "wildness" even after years as lab specimens on a university campus. To Lehrman, who watched them go through their typical breeding behavior stage by stage, these questions occurred:

Could the sequence — courting, nesting, mating, incubating, brooding — be stopped or started by changes in body chemistry? And what could thereby be learned about the behavior of ring doves?

His set of experiments made use of hormones, powerful chemical substances that are naturally produced in the bodies of animals. Hormones, secreted by certain glands, are commonly released into the bloodstream, passing from one organ, tissue, cell to another. Much research work has been done by artificially injecting animals with so-called sex hormones, androgens and estrogens, known respectively as male and female hormones. These substances have strong influences on "target organs" involved in sexual behavior.

In a brilliant series of experiments with doves, Lehrman probed the place of hormones in the total pattern of bird behavior. A bird reacts to outside stimuli at every step of its breeding cycle. It responds to the mate, to nesting materials, to the nest itself, to eggs — all in sequence, moving from one behavior to the next. Each step is accompanied by changes in its inner hormone production.

Skilled with the scalpel, Lehrman was able through

surgery to cut off the natural flow of hormones. The effect was to break the chain of breeding behavior. Birds without the necessary hormone supplies lost interest in mate, nest, eggs. None of the usual stimuli from outside could induce breeding behavior. But once the missing hormones were restored by injection, Lehrman's doves resumed their normal reproductive patterns.

Lehrman concluded: "Courtship, nest-building, incubation and feeding of the young can all be induced in ring doves by the injection of hormones equivalent to those secreted by the bird's own glands at appropriate stages in the cycle."

A good many mysteries remain about these substances which, in tiny quantities, control a great deal of male-female behavior. In chemical makeup, the sex hormones found in doves and prairie dogs, monkeys and human beings hardly differ. But in various species these chemical agents are linked with widely differing behaviors.

Are hormones the secret makers of behavior — or are they produced in response to stimuli from outside? Are they cause or effect — or both? In some respects there is still a chicken-and-egg mystery as to which comes first, the activity or the hormones. As Lehrman pointed out, "The very hormones which induce the successive changes in behavior are themselves induced by stimuli coming from the environment, including those arising from the bird and its mate, such as song, the nest, eggs, etc."

Sex hormones are key factors in preparing the young of both sexes for their adult sexual functions. They are also important in the development of adults for breeding, in preparing males and females so that they can jointly complete the intricate processes of sexual reproduction.

Hormones are at work as migratory species prepare for their journeys to breeding sites. Males are stirred by hormones to acts of rivalry and to mating behavior. Hormones control the breeding cycles of females so that they become capable of producing young only at fixed intervals. This so-called estrus period may be very brief. Some mammalian females are "in heat" only once a year, but most estrous cycles recur more often. Rats and rabbits are out of breeding condition for very short intervals.

Courtship displays that begin the mating season set the hormones flowing. In turn, it is the influence of hormones that brings on the colorful courting garb of many species, the elaborate displays and the many kinds of signals that result in pairing.

As the breeding cycle continues, the reproductive cells, sperm and eggs, are produced under the guidance of hormones. Certain organs increase in size and activity. Sex hormones are responsible also for the development of organs that provide food for the young. Lehrman has described the crop in ring doves, the organ from which the young are fed crop milk. Since both parents feed the young, the crops of both males and females triple in size during brooding. The egg-laying organs of the female increase fourfold in size and weight. At the same time, the female also develops what is called a brood patch. This is an area of skin which loses its feathers and is located where the mother's body warmth can best be delivered to eggs and nestlings. In those bird species in which males typically sit on the eggs, the action of hormones also creates the same useful patch of bare skin.

Small traces of hormones may bring on astounding changes. Added quantities beyond a certain level may have no visible effect on behavior at all. Nor do hormones necessarily act in predictable ways on the two sexes. The injection of so-called male hormone in a female may bring on a display of aggression. And in some species in which males care for the young, the adding of those hormones found more plentifully in females may increase these nurturing tendencies. However, there is no rule that says the use of specific hormones will bring on behavior commonly considered to be either "masculine" or "feminine" — or necessarily change any conduct at all.

Hormones have become a useful experimental tool. They are one more added factor in the intricate combinations that can produce behavior when all work together.

Students of animal behavior can look back less than half a century to a time when it was widely believed that all behavior was either "learned" or "unlearned." That may have been a comforting idea in its simplicity. But modern scientists in this field say the old idea really tells us nothing about behavior.

Back in the 1920s, some early psychologists shaped their own oversimplified view in claiming that behavior could be totally regulated through control of the environment. That notion has also been seriously questioned.

The student of animal behavior today finds himself peering into a deep, half-dark pool in which only a few clear shapes emerge within the swirl of waters. Most of what he can glimpse is still unclear. And each bit of information gained is only a highlight against the murky depths beyond.

Few investigators of behavior believe they will ever discover a set of laws that will explain everything. They are dealing with the complexities of genes and chromosomes, stimuli and living responses, sensory organs and nervous systems, bodily fluids and structures, in all their ceaseless movement and change. A store of information is growing about some species, along with ideas about what is called typical behavior.

This still doesn't tell us much about individual differences, which range widely in every species. As this new science frees itself from old ideas about innate uniform behavior, it becomes increasingly possible to understand the unique qualities of the single organism.

Male and female relationships have been closely studied by some investigators. But most of the research so far deals with reproductive behavior, which is a vital function but still only part of the life cycle of animals. Sexual behavior is itself an intricate subject, as yet dimly understood. Some scientists have found it useful to go back to the very origins of this kind of behavior, back into worlds in which life is simpler and sexes do not even exist.

7 · Watcher by the Sea

The seas abound with living forms that recall the origin of life on this planet. Rachel Carson, marine biologist and superb writer, was fascinated with these surviving relics of remote ages.

Born an inlander, she lived her entire adult life at the seaside. For her, the ocean was "the place of our dim ancestral beginnings." And as a research scientist, the sea appeared to her to be a revealing showcase of evolution. "Life first drifted in the shallow waters," she wrote, "reproducing, evolving, yielding that endlessly varied stream of living things that has surged through time and space to occupy the earth."

Evolution has been described as a reproductive process, centered on the success or failure of species to maintain their own kind. And in the three books about the sea which she wrote in the 1940s and 1950s, Rachel Carson described with deep insight the wide range of structures and strategies which sea and shore animals developed for producing new generations.

Many of the simplest creatures, single-celled, live in watery habitats. The bloblike amoeba, best known among them, has been described so often as "multiplying by division," halving itself into two separate individuals. That method of reproduction has survived to this day among many species. These individuals are well able to reproduce without the help of partners. The members of such species are very much alike. They are neither male nor female, and their behavior has nothing to do with sex.

Their way of creating new generations without any pairing or mating has the merit of simplicity. But in the long course of evolution, reproduction by a single parent proved to have serious disadvantages. And while the surviving one-sex species may be considered a success, a great many others have failed and vanished.

The change from one-sex to two-sex patterns was a slow one. The gradualness of it may still be seen in the countless species which remain caught in midcourse between one type of reproduction and the other. Rachel Carson studied these biological types in habitats that display another kind of transition — the evolutionary process by which many sea animals moved onto the land.

"When we go down to the low-tide line," she wrote, "we enter a world that is as old as the earth itself — a primeval meeting place of the elements of earth and water, a place of compromise and conflict and eternal change."

Here are species that continue themselves in a variety of

ways. In some there is no distinction between male and female. The young may have a single parent — or sometimes two. Some animals are treelike, with the offspring appearing as buds that drift off and go their own way. In other cases, a single parent may lay eggs which do not unite with sperm—but the new generation appears nonetheless.

Most astonishing of all are the species which shift back and forth between one method of reproduction and another. At times, jellyfish scatter their male and female sex cells into the seas, on the chance that some sperm and eggs will get together. These same adult jellyfish will be seen at other times growing buds on their bodies which become offshoots and reach toward adulthood.

When a member of a common variety of Atlantic shrimp begins life, he is definitely a male. The females are all older. And in his early years, the male is able to fertilize their eggs. However, as the male shrimp ages, "he" gradually becomes a "she," capable only of laying eggs and not of fertilizing them. In describing the type of snail known as a limpet, Rachel Carson pointed out that "probably all young limpets are males, later transforming to females."

She studied the small, reddish brown starfish, Linkia, which breaks apart, with each of its star rays growing additional parts and becoming a complete new animal. "These divisions seem to be a method of reproduction practiced by the young," she wrote, "for adult animals cease to fragment and produce eggs."

In this world between the tides, she roamed widely, a slight, quiet woman, usually alone throughout long hours of patient study. Along the Maine coast, near the marine research laboratory at Woods Hole, Massachusetts, on the beaches of the Carolinas and later in the Florida Keys, she studied the offshore species. At times she waded in icy waters with magnifier in hand until she was blue with cold. She spent hours in hidden rocky caves, accessible only at low tide. Or else she might lie stretched full length at the side of a tidepool, quietly examining its varied forms of animal life.

"I can't think of any more exciting place to be," she wrote, "than down in the low-tide world when the ebb tide falls very early in the morning and the world is full of salt smell, and the sound of water, and the softness of fog."

Rachel Carson was a modest woman quite unprepared for the fame which her writing brought. She was astounded by the worldwide excitement caused by her book *Silent Spring*, which revealed how the balances of nature were being destroyed through the reckless use of chemical agents.

For much of her life, Rachel Carson was a keenly observant seeker of knowledge at the seashore. Other oceanographers may have gathered greater quantities of technical data or developed more complex theories. But no one has caught the marine life rhythms in the way Rachel Carson has.

She was finely tuned to the interplay between land and sea, sensitive to the pulsebeats of the shore habitats. Here, many tempos rise and fall. Tides are daily events, varying throughout the year. The regular return of the full moon is yet another bringer of change to the organisms that live in 'the transition zones of the waterfront. Every living thing responds to the cycle of the seasons, which influences its reproduction. Slower still is the rhythmic time scale by which generations live and die.

The shore species here "belongs now to the land, now to the sea," Rachel Carson wrote. "Animals belonging to quite unrelated groups throughout the whole range of sea life spawn according to a definitely fixed rhythm that may coincide with the full moon or the new moon or its quarters."

One kind of snail waits for the waves of the spring tides to cast its eggs into the sea. A clamlike mollusk spawns heavily between the full and new moon, but avoids the first quarter. Certain fishes come ashore on the surf in order to spawn, but only at a certain phase of the moon. Species of sea worms produce their young only in the powerful autumn tides.

Early one midsummer morning, Rachel Carson padded softly across a great mud flat on a Florida island cove down to the edge of the retreating sea. The tide had partly erased the tracks of land mammals and birds who had come earlier to feed on shore animals. In that moment, Rachel Carson felt a strong sense of "the interchangeability of land and sea in this marginal world of the shore, and of the links between the life of the two." She later wrote, "There was also an awareness of the past and of the continuing flow of time, obliterating much that had gone before, as the sea had that morning washed away the tracks of the birds."

In these natural habitats she studied the reproductive behavior of species about which little is known. Could it be possible that oysters shift back and forth from male to female once or twice a year, she wondered? What of the floating moon jellies, in which the new generations alternate, one produced by budding and the next by eggs and sperm? Or the sea hares, shaggy, bottle-shaped creatures, each individual functioning "as either sex, or as both"?

A blue-backed, hard-shelled species typified for her the clear-cut development of reproduction by two distinct sexes. She saw these animals living densely together as "cities of mussels," washed by the pounding surf.

"The female mussels discharge the eggs in a continuing, almost endless stream of short little rod-like masses — hundreds, thousands, millions of cells, each potentially an adult mussel," she wrote. At the same time, the water becomes cloudy with the milt poured into the sea by the male mussels — uncounted individual sperm cells swimming free.

"Dozens of them cluster about a single egg, pressing

against it, seeking entrance," Rachel Carson wrote. "But one male cell, and only one is successful. With the entrance of this first sperm cell, an instantaneous physical change takes place in the outer membranes of the egg and from this moment it cannot again be penetrated by a spermatozoan. In less than the interval between a low and a high tide, the egg has been transformed into a little ball of cells. . . ." Suddenly, a young mussel is entering the tideland world.

To Rachel Carson, the sea's edge disclosed "the spectacle of life in all its varied manifestations as it has appeared, evolved and sometimes died out." Clearly, a turning point in the survival of species was the coming of sexuality, the reproduction of new generations by parents in pairs.

Many water-living species made their move shoreward millions of years ago. The air of the planet had then become more humid, the land less dry and barren. Somehow the shore beckoned those aquatic types which were more adventuresome and better adapted to the new environment.

For Rachel Carson, the small, cone-shelled snails called periwinkles were typical of "the first of the sea creatures pressing up to the threshold of the land." Related periwinkles of several kinds which she observed in habitats very close to each other on the New England coast are differently adapted to the separate shore levels on which they live. They display a remarkable range of sexual behavior.

The most numerous, called the common periwinkle, are found midway between the low and high tide lines. This is a slow-moving animal that may simply attach itself for life to a bare stone or seaweed or moss-covered rock. In some ways, this species has evolved shore-living habits. But for breeding, the common periwinkle returns to a pattern typical of sea creatures. "It still sheds eggs into the sea," wrote Rachel Carson, "and so is not ready for land life." When and if these eggs are ripened, the young come drifting back to the shore on the tides.

A cousin species, the smooth periwinkle, is in some ways even more of a sea being. This periwinkle is not often left high and dry by the receding tides. It lives attached to rockweeds which remain wet and dripping when they are not under water. The smooth periwinkle female fastens its eggs to the weeds, where they are fertilized by the male. The new generations never leave the weeds.

A third member of this close kinship of snails is the rough periwinkle, found somewhat higher on the shore but still well within reach of the salt spray and the tidewaters. In producing its young, this species has broken its ties with the ocean.

"The rough periwinkle sends no young into the sea," Rachel Carson wrote. "Instead it is a viviparous species and the eggs, each encased within a cocoon, are held within the mother's body while they develop. The contents of the cocoon nourish the young snail until finally it breaks through the egg capsule and then emerges from the mother's body, a completely shelled little creature about the size of a grain of finely-ground coffee."

The shells of land-living snails easily betray their sea origins. As Rachel Carson observed, "All snails that are now terrestrial came of marine ancestry, their forebears having at one time made the transitional crossing of the shore." Land snails not only reveal trends toward new types of reproduction. These animals have also developed ways of protecting male and female sex cells from the dryness of wind and the sun's heat, and from many other land-based perils. Both sexes exist within each individual. The adults do not fertilize their own eggs. Instead two snails come together, their bodies tightly joined. Then both transfer male sperm, each fertilizing the other's eggs.

Fertilization of eggs within the body of the parent developed as one of those major turns in the course of evolution. Dry land species required this means of reproducing if they were to survive. A number of aquatic animals also evolved in this direction.

In some species, internal fertilization is carried out without complex organs. The flowerlike sea anemone has a body formed like a cup. Eggs are shed into this container while sperm from another parent are deposited in it as well, and fertilization takes place within the cup.

Crude as it is, even this means of fertilization is far less wasteful than the almost random scattering of eggs by most fishes and amphibians. Some marine species lay millions of unfertilized eggs in a single spawning. The chances of their being reached by male sex cells are small, and relatively few survive.

A great many fishes, reptiles and birds and a few mammals lay eggs which have been internally fertilized. These eggs may be hatched by either parent or by both, depending on the species. Still another reproductive pattern which evolved among some fishes and a great many higher species is the retaining of the fertilized egg in the body of the parent until it is ready to be born alive.

All of these variations in reproductive methods are part of a wide range of behaviors seen among males and females. Breeding habits of different species are seldom uniform or predictable. A striking example is the case of the sea horse.

This animal has been described has having the head of a horse, the tail of a monkey and the belly pouch of the kangaroo. However, it is not both sexes that have the pouch — only the male. He is approached by the female in an elaborate courtship dance. The she–sea horse is the more colorful of the two both in adornments and in per-

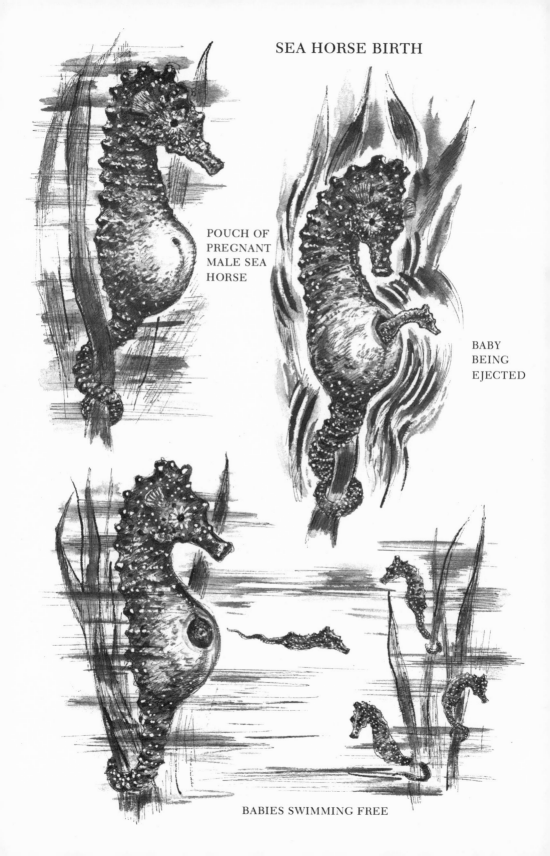

SEA HORSE BIRTH

POUCH OF
PREGNANT
MALE SEA
HORSE

BABY
BEING
EJECTED

BABIES SWIMMING FREE

formance. From the sunless depths, they rise toward the surface, the two intertwined and swaying as they go.

At the moment of mating, the male offers his open pouch, into which the female inserts a tube through which a number of eggs are delivered. At once, the male pours his sperm into the pouch, which then closes to seal in the fertilized eggs. By the time the embryos develop, the pouch has swelled, stretched almost to bursting. At last the father is ready to deliver the babies. He shows much excitement, straining and turning pale and doubling up in a series of spasms. One by one, the young seem to explode from the pouch, each swimming off on its own.

The sea horse is no more strange in its behavior than are thousands of species which have found their own separate paths to survival. The opportunity for these countless and diverse adaptations was opened to them by sexual reproduction. It is only when they have two parents instead of one that offspring win the ability to diverge into a great many evolutionary byways.

Single-sex creatures are dull in their sameness. Like parent, like young. The offspring inherit the same genetic material that the single parent inherited from its single parent. And there is only a slight chance that the new generation will contain any outstanding members.

The sameness is dangerous. Should the climate suddenly shift or the water or air change in chemistry or a new predator appear, an entire population or a species might be wiped out without a single hardy survivor. One-sex reproduction does not favor the appearance of extraordinary groups or individuals who can succeed in an environment that has suddenly turned hostile and perilous. The new generations are scarcely any better able to cope with difficult conditions than were the previous ones.

That situation is completely altered when two distinct sexes appear, and when reproduction involves the fusing of sex cells from two parents. Out of this combination a unique individual emerges. Such an offspring is different in makeup from either parent, even though it has characteristics of both.

Those species that developed the two-sex form of breeding gained not only reproductive success but also new freedom for change. With their offspring containing a mix of genes from two sources, these species improved their power to survive. In oncoming generations, new traits could arise through combinations and recombinations of hereditary material. And features which might prove to be advantageous could spread more widely and rapidly through entire populations. A species reproducing sexually could offer a great range of genetic mixtures to withstand any harsh new demands of the environment. Natural selection clearly favored the types of animals that have developed the method of paired breeding.

The sexual mode of life has won out in the sea. It has proved advantageous on the land. And it has been selected by nature in what Rachel Carson saw as the most challenging of environments, the endlessly changing seashore. The triumph of sexuality is seen in those species that she described so vividly, living in what she called "a place that demands every bit of adaptability living things can muster."

On a midsummer Sunday morning in 1949, Rachel Carson had a friendly phone call from a book editor. The caller was puzzled about an experience that had followed a weekend gathering at her Cape Cod home.

Her guests, the editor said, had taken a morning stroll and found the beach strewn with horseshoe crabs. Thinking the creatures had been stranded by the storm of the previous night, the visitors returned the crabs to the sea. Was this a proper thing to do? And would Rachel Carson perhaps write a book which would enlighten readers in such matters?

Amused, the scientist-author explained about horseshoe

crabs, offering a few facts which she would later expand in her book *The Edge of the Sea.* In trying to be helpful, the guests at Cape Cod had unintentionally interrupted the normal mating patterns of the crabs.

"On a summer night when the moon is full," Rachel Carson later wrote, "the sea and the swelling tide and a creature of the ancient shore conspire to work primeval magic on many of the beaches from Maine to Florida. On such a night the horseshoe crabs move in, just as they did under a Paleozoic moon — just as they have been doing through all the hundreds of millions of years since then — coming out of the sea to dig their nests in the wet sand and spawn."

She described the males also emerging out of the surf, crawling up the beach to fertilize the eggs. Finally, left behind by the adult crabs, the fertilized eggs are covered with sand by the incoming tide. "A month after the egg-laying the embryos will be ready for life," Rachel Carson explained. "Then the high tides of another full moon will wash away the sand of the nest. The turbulence of the rising tide will cause the egg membranes to split, releasing the young crabs to a life of their own over the shallow shores of the bays and sounds."

In their roles as partners in reproduction, male and female horseshoe crabs act out distinct behavior patterns, as do the countless other species of two-sexed animals.

What are males and females? In many species, they are strikingly different from each other in size, shape and color. In other species, the members of the two sexes look very much alike. By their behaviors, some animals can be readily identified as females, while their male counterparts have distinct habits of their own. However, in many other species, it is not readily apparent that the two sexes act differently. There is no biological rule that says a female is the bearer of the young or keeper of the nest or that she is necessarily shy or soft or submissive. Nor are the traits of strength, aggressiveness and dominance peculiar to males throughout the animal kingdom.

The biologist defines the female only as a producer of the kind of sex cells known as eggs. The male can be described with accuracy as the source of spermatozoa or sperm cells. Both egg and sperm cells are formed in organs within the bodies of females and males which are called gonads. The two types of germ or sex cells differ in many ways. Eggs cells tend to be larger, food-filled and more stationary. In general, the sperm cells are relatively tiny in size, and more active. Typically, the long-tailed sperm swims through fluid and may collide with an egg and penetrate it. This begins the process of fertilization and the development of an embryo.

The basic functional differences between male and female relate to reproduction. In a good many species, the distinct sexual features develop during periods in the lives of animals when they are capable of producing young. Certain sexual characteristics may appear briefly and then disappear until the breeding season of the following year. The two sexes may not differ at all in their digestive, nervous, circulatory, muscular, skeletal, or respiratory systems, nor in any activity other than that of reproduction.

The future sex of an animal is usually determined at the moment when its two germ cells become one and the combination of genes spells out either a male or female identity. But Rachel Carson studied a number of species in which sex determination is by no means so fixed or clear.

One of these was Anguilla, the common freshwater eel, which goes to the sea to spawn. Scientists differently interpret their puzzling sexuality and the meaning of the fact that those eels usually found in estuaries and river mouths close to the sea are males, whereas females commonly appear far upstream in inland waters. Perhaps the two sexes begin life by seeking out these differing habitats. Another view is that early environments play a large part in deciding the sex of individual eels.

In addition to inner differences in their gonads and hormonal systems, males and females may often be distinguished by their external sexual organs. These differ especially in those species which fertilize eggs internally. Somewhere along the gradual time flow of uncounted generations, animals began to develop special means for the safe transfer of sex cells from one parent to the other. Most of these adaptations take the form of a protruding male tube and a female duct.

In the act of copulation, the bodies of male and female are coupled together. The male organ, or penis, is inserted in the female organ, or vagina. Sex cells are thus transferred with a minimum of danger. In some species, sperm are delivered in a sealed package. Or they may be enclosed within a thick layer of some jellylike substance. However, sperm are most commonly delivered from male to female in a fluid medium through which the sperm swim to reach the eggs.

Among the so-called secondary sexual organs are some that are specialized for the feeding of the young. Among mammals, the females have one or more pairs of glands which produce milk for the offspring. In some bird species, both males and females secrete milk within their bodies for the nourishment of the young.

As to behavior, the members of the two sexes may differ in courting, mating, nesting and nurturing conduct. They may have some clear division of labor between them. However, these differences of activity may occur only during the mating season and be absent during the rest of the life cycle.

Such patterns of sexual behavior, seen in species ranging from insects to human beings, have proven to be successful in producing new generations. Sexual reproduction is an act of cooperation by two organisms. In such cooperative behavior, the basis is laid for family and social life. The sharing often begins in the very social activities which first bring mates together. And male-female relationships may continue long after the breeding period.

At the outset of pairing, members of the two sexes identify each other and reveal their readiness for mating. This is especially significant in those species in which the time for breeding is very brief. In all mammals except the higher primates, mating takes place only during a clearly defined period, when the female is in estrus, or heat. The estrous cycle is the rhythm of the periodic ripening and shedding of unfertilized eggs. Only after the egg is shed is the female desirous and capable of mating.

During the estrus period, female mammals ordinarily emit odors which are mating signals to the males of their species. But such signals are sometimes not detected. And if males seem to be constantly pursuing mates, they are ordinarily finding out whether the females are ready to mate.

In meeting the tests of natural selection, insects and fishes, amphibians and mammals, reptiles and birds have developed their own successful ways to reproduce. Rachel Carson described the typical female mussel releasing 25 million eggs at a single spawning, an effort that is the price its species pays for its continuity.

By contrast, the mammalian pair may develop only one or two offspring at a time. Mammal species have evolved toward providing highly protected conditions for their young.

8 · The Secret of the Pack

Mammals offer their newborn safety, food, warmth and all the comforts of home. And for all this, the female commonly bears the main responsibility.

The young of mammals are born alive after they have been carried in the bodies of their mothers. It is ordinarily the female parent who protects the infants during their period of helplessness. In most mammal species, fathers wander off after mating or after the birth of offspring. Some never return. In many cases, the mother is vigilant lest the father come back to eat the young. After breeding, the male may even be treated as an enemy and the litter vigorously protected from him.

From a strictly human viewpoint, this kind of fatherly behavior may appear vile and outrageous. However, biologists do not ordinarily make moral judgments about such conduct. Rabbits, which commonly have more off-spring than they can individually care for, are not "poor mothers." And those mammal males that take on the full parental role in raising orphaned babies that may not even be their own are not rated as "good fathers." The male and female roles seen in the animal world are not morally determined nor wilfully chosen. They are adaptive and have evolved as answers — by species equipped in certain ways — to the special problems of living in specific environments.

Mammals evolved as hairy, warm-blooded species from the scaly, cold-blooded reptiles that dominated the earth a hundred million years ago. There are many features that now distinguish the behavior of mammals from that of their reptilian ancestors. These include differences in family and social life.

The reptile parent is ordinarily little involved with its young. Snakes' eggs are usually left to hatch on their own and the live-born offspring fend for themselves. In mammals, adaptations for survival have brought about different kinds of relationships between the parents and the young. These, in turn, set special patterns of male-female behavior throughout the mammalian species.

Nurture for the young is, of course, common in many lower animals. Songbirds which feed their nestlings with insects make several hundred food-gathering trips in a day. Among sea catfish, the male gathers up the marble-sized eggs and incubates and broods them in his mouth, fasting all the while. In laying their eggs, many insects provide their offspring with a ready source of food when they are born. Some animals like the salmon defy death in order to reach safe spawning grounds.

However, the mammal parent may spend most of its total life span bearing and caring for offspring. Nurture is usually long and arduous. An elephant mother devotes twenty months to carrying its baby, which does not mature for another thirty years!

Relationships between adult males and females revolve around the breeding of new generations. The mammal pattern of life is often determined by the condition of the young at birth and the size of the litter. Some mammals, like most birds, bring into the world offspring that may be utterly helpless. Of course, this is not the case with mammal species that are constantly grazing. From the moment they rise on unsteady legs, baby buffalo, deer, zebras must move fast in order to keep up with the migrating herd. Hares, porcupines, guinea pigs are fairly well developed at birth. However, these and other mammal species depend on their parent or parents for protection and learning the ways of their kind while they mature.

Young bears depend on their mothers for two years. Chimpanzees are still clinging to their parents' bodies at the age of five. Sightless and deaf at birth, wolf pups are also weak, each weighing about a pound. They can whine and even yelp. But their body movements are limited to a slow, draggy crawl. For months, the mother remains with the litter constantly.

The wolf mother begins nesting preparations weeks before her litter appears. She may dig several elaborate dens, sometimes with the help of her mate and other adult members of the pack. The wild rabbit lines its birthing nest with soft fur from its own body. While waiting for her young to appear, the lioness plucks hair from her underside with her teeth so that the cubs may readily find the suckling nipples.

The period of carrying the fetus, or gestation, varies

greatly. An opossum delivers its litter in two weeks. But the young are then carried in the pouch for a longer period, followed by another lengthy phase in which the young are borne on the mother opossum's back. The rat has a short period of gestation — which permits it to have litters very often. A camel carries its fetus for more than a year. Female sperm whales give birth after sixteen months.

At its moment of birth, the mammalian infant is commonly licked from head to tail by its mother. It is now believed by scientists that this is more than just washing. Experimental work with mammal babies shows that they have a deep need for nurturing of this kind. Licking, nuzzling, touching seem to be vitally necessary — and those infants which do not get enough of it fail to develop properly as adults. The newborn may also have trouble maintaining their body temperature, and close contact helps.

It is the nature of all mammals that they are breast-feeders. The adult female has mammary glands which produce milk, hence the name "mammal." There may be as many as twelve pairs of these glands, depending on the size of the normal litter for that species. A protruding nipple gives each offspring access to a nourishing supply of food.

Milk from a mammalian mother is remarkably rich and healthful. The first supplies of mother's milk for the newborn contain chemical substances that protect the offspring from diseases of infancy. Marine mammals are known to produce an especially abundant supply for their breast-feeding young. The porpoise mother has a special set of muscles and pumps the milk through the nipple to its feeding baby at a fast rate. Thirty gallons at a single feeding are delivered to its young by the female gray whale.

Among the mammals, it is the primate monkeys and apes that wait the longest before weaning the young and changing their diet to adult foods. In the case of chimpanzees, the breast-feeding period may last as long as three years.

The meat-eating species must supply their young with food from the time they are weaned until the time when they learn to hunt. Such mammal parents teach predator skills, mostly by example. Gradually, the young develop strength and speed in climbing, running, swimming.

With this period of learning and experience, the long nurturing process comes to an end. When they are half-grown, many of the young carnivores are ready to join the communal hunt, even though they may not as yet take part directly in the kill. The future survival of both the young males and females depends on how well they master the skills of securing fresh meat. Even the wolf cub may starve unless it is trained to hunt.

Scientists trying to explain the behavior of wolves are plagued by a troublesome figure — the big bad wolf in "Little Red Riding Hood." The public image of the species has been deeply influenced by this familiar children's story and by many other myths, folk legends and tall tales.

Amiable, devoted, sociable, loyal — such adjectives are seldom applied to wolves. And yet one of America's foremost authorities on this species, Adolph Murie, could say, "The strongest impression remaining with me after watching the wolves on numerous occasions was their friendliness."

In the late 1930s, Murie began a series of studies which probably saved the Alaska wolves from extinction and led to the protection of many other mammalian species as well. Settlers in the Northwest had for many years been carrying on a systematic slaughter of wolves on the ground that they were killing off too many game animals. Bounties for dead wolves were being offered in many sections of the United States and Canada.

Murie, an outstanding naturalist, warned that the antiwolf campaign would not only wipe out the species but also upset the natural balance. He was able to get the

United States government to sponsor a scientific study of Alaskan wildlife with himself in charge of investigating the wolf as a predator of wild Dall sheep.

His studies in the Mount McKinley area were carried on by untiring personal observation. Throughout the seasons he tracked the wolves, probed their feeding patterns through examining the remainders of their kills and the contents of their waste products. The wolves, he learned, were in fact killers of moose, caribou and mountain sheep. But their predation served to strengthen the ecology and served the processes of natural selection. Murie revealed for the first time some remarkable features in the home life of wolves.

On a May morning in 1939, Murie spotted wolf tracks in the fresh snow along the East Fork River. A mile of tracking brought him face to face with a large black male wolf. The animal's howling and nervous behavior set Murie looking for something which he found, a den containing newborn pups. The enraged female soon joined the male in loud howling complaints against the intruder.

Murie realized that the parents might now move the den to a new location and he would lose the opportunity to study this wolf family. "I could not make matters much worse," he later wrote, "so I wriggled into the burrow to investigate the young." In the third of a series of chambers he found six pups, about a week old. He took one back to his own camp with him for closer study.

The wolf family did not move out in spite of Murie's surprise visit. In fact, the naturalist was able to keep these wolves under close scrutiny for the next months. Twice he observed them all night long, and one other continuous vigil lasted thirty-three hours.

One morning, two males he had not seen before appeared outside the den. Several days later, another female, all black, appeared. In late July another male joined the group, making seven adults in all. Murie could not determine whether the newcomers had any kinship to the first pair. But it was clear to him that all of these adults and pups together had now become a stable family group.

They moved and hunted, fed and played together. They formed a common defense against danger. And when another wolf tried to join them, they acted together in chasing off the stranger. One of the members of the enlarged wolf group was obviously somewhat older, and Murie called him "Grandpa." The second female acted like an "aunt" toward the pups. On three occasions, the pups' mother joined the males in the night hunt while the "aunt" stayed with the litter.

In this pack the four extra males were described by Murie as "bachelors." They were unmated. One of these males was a tall, rangy wolf who seemed to be "lord and master" of the entire group. It was not the father of the pups but this larger male who appeared to be the leader. He gave the signals in the strategy of the hunt, trotted jauntily in the lead of the pack while the others deferred to him and sometimes cowered before him.

Murie's detailed notes on this tightly knit pack revealed features in the lives of wolves that had never before been recorded but have been reaffirmed many times since the naturalist's studies in Mount McKinley Park. The small wolf pack, centered on a mated pair and its pups, has now been studied many times as a pattern of living common not only for wolves but for other pack-hunting animals.

Such a group depends on close and friendly relationships between its members and on a high level of cooperation and communication among them. Murie marveled at the "good feeling" among the wolves of the East Fork River pack. He saw few quarrels. During the period when the mother was confined to the den with her young, the other adults brought part of the kill back to her. All of the adults took part in caring for the pups, bringing food and joining in lively play with them. By early fall, all the adults and pups were taking part in the hunt together, the young learning by watchfulness, imitation and practice.

"Considerable ceremony often precedes the departure for the hunt," Murie wrote. "Usually there is a general get-together and much tail-wagging." After the hunt, howling was an activity in which all joined vigorously.

Later studies have shown that wolf pack size is adaptive, depending largely on hunting habits. If the common prey is the caribou, then the wolf pack is formed large enough to bring down the quarry — and small enough so that the entire pack can feed on a single kill.

Among the wolves Murie studied, it was the caribou that constituted the chief natural prey. This type of herding reindeer is a large, fleet animal with hooves that are far more dangerous than its antlers. The wolf pack is constantly on the lookout for a sick or disabled and old animal that is alone, or for a female and its young that are unable to keep up with the herd.

The hunting tactics involve great skill and common effort. The wolves tire out the prey by spelling each other during the chase. Once they have cornered a cow and calf, they try warily to separate the two — and if they succeed the battle is soon over. After they have inflicted serious wounds, the pack may wait patiently for hours while their quarry is slowly weakened by loss of blood.

The hunt seems to create the social bond which keeps the pack together. Through most of the year, the wolves live in their pack, but in the early spring they appear as pairs. Murie observed the following year that the pair at East Fork River were still together. There would be a new litter, and a different combination of unmated adults would become part of the pack.

Another year passed. Now two pairs of the pack's members mated. For a time, the mothers tended their litters in separate dens. But in late spring, Murie watched one of them carry her cubs to the other den. The two families lived together as a communal group throughout the summer. What a howling chorus there was that winter when the enlarged pack joined in its first hunt!

To a naturalist like Murie, forms of group life were to be seen everywhere across the wilderness areas he knew so well. And yet he saw in the mammals something far advanced beyond the colonies of insects, the schools of stream fishes or the flocks of snow geese flying overhead. Far more developed than any of these groupings were the social forms of mammals.

Murie studied the herds of prey species such as the deer and caribou. His research probed the lives of such group hunters as cougars, coyotes and foxes, the free-living and powerful "cats" of the Alaskan mountains, the herds of seals on the offshore islands and the colonies of rodents, bats and beavers. In the social lives of these animals could be seen a high degree of mutual support, sharing, the expression of emotion, subtle communication and a sense of group identity.

Among these many social mammals, however, few seemed to reach the cohesive and cooperative group living of the wolves. The wolf pack was more than a mere hunting society, gathered for travel, feeding and defense. The pack was held together by strong bonds among all the animals. At its center was the mated pair.

For animals, the mating season is a time of learning. As we have seen, the long courtships of many birds and fishes are periods of fact-finding in which mates find and find out about each other.

However, most mammals do not go through extended and elaborate behaviors in order to discover the species and sex of a possible mate and its readiness for copulation. Mammals can ordinarily receive such information from their sense of smell. By odors, mammals are able to distinguish not only their own kind but also members of familiar groups and even individuals. And although a male may receive a direct mating invitation from a female, he already knows when she is in estrus by her scent.

For mating mammals there are ordinarily few preliminaries. The bull moose may sound his bass rutting call. Male rabbits put on a wild display of running and leaping. Fighting between males is a pre-mating ritual in many mammal species. The victor is not necessarily the strongest but the one best able to terrorize his opponent with a show of ferocity. Antlers, horns, fangs and hooves are used for fighting and threatening. Some males use bristling hair, puffed-up chests and angry sounds in order to impress their rivals and any watchful females. Most of these mammalian courting behaviors, however, are carried on during the short breeding season and are therefore also very brief.

Wolves and other related species have much longer periods of pairing. At the age of one, young wolves are already looking for mates. They will not even be capable of breeding for at least another year. But the extremely early courting of wolves is a key not only to their pairing but also to their family and pack patterns of life.

Studies of wolves show that they tend to make their final choices of mates only when they become fully adult. Both males and females seem to develop strong mate preferences. And when the pair finally get together to produce a litter, they ordinarily have formed a partnership that is continuous. Typically, they establish an enduring bond that may last for a lifetime.

Adolph Murie's careful observations showed that pairs den together from one season to the next. And rematings are rare unless one partner dies. Similar conduct has been noted among cougars, foxes, coyotes.

The mammal act of mating itself may appear at times as a display of aggression between male and female. However, this is likely to be part of the difficult and intricate process by which the pair is coordinated into just the right condition for copulation. In the moment of mating, the two partners are tightly joined to insure the completion of the sexual act. The male commonly grasps the female with limbs, tail or teeth. Biting and holding the female's neck skin is commonly a necessary part of coupling. The sexual organs of wolves and other species swell in such a way that the mating pairs are physically locked together and remain so for several minutes after sexual intercourse has been completed.

Among wolves and other mammalian species, the female going into mating condition is commonly treated with care and deference. The pregnant female or the mother with young is cared for not only by her mate but also by other members of the herd or pack.

In some mammal species, males and females live separately except for the brief breeding period. New pairs may form every year, seasonally, or for each breeding occurrence. Among lions and other large cat species there appears to be no close attachment between individuals, even though males and females live within a clearly defined group. Most bears are also uncommitted to each other. Some burrowing types do not have much of a family home life. In fact, moles commonly enter their burrows backward — supposedly to make sure that they are not being followed by a member of the opposite sex. Not all mammals are as sociable as wolves.

Because the social patterns of wolves are exceptional, a number of young scientists have been attracted in recent years to the study of these burly, free-ranging predators. One of these is David L. Mech, a Midwestern American who is tracking the tradition of Murie.

Thirty-five years after Murie's pioneer research at Mount McKinley, Mech has the advantage of modern techniques. He can locate and observe wolves from a small airplane and is often able to watch the full pack in action from aloft. He catches wolves and fastens on each a collar containing a radio transmitter which is then monitored for a variety of information. But the hardworking Mech also spends much of his time as close to the wolves as he can get, usually with camera in hand.

The locale of Mech's research is northern Minnesota. He made a lengthy and detailed study of the wild wolves of Isle Royale. Here he observed the social habits of wolves as adaptive behaviors that fit naturally into a life pattern of hunting in groups.

"The personality of the wolf is related most directly to the animal's social nature," Mech pointed out. "An ability to form emotional attachments to other individuals results in the formation of the pack as the basic unit of wolf society."

Such bonds are apparent in the mated pair, in the relationships between parents and young and in the unity among all members of the pack. Commonly, the pack contains fewer than eight members. These include a pair of breeding adults, pups and extra adults. A "lone" wolf, unmated, tends to attach itself to a pack. This male or female may join as a low-ranking member. But the newcomer becomes an integrated part of the group, loyal and cooperative. In time, such extra males and females may find mates within the pack.

Mech insists that the wolf tends to be nonviolent and docile. However, male and female wolves are fierce in harassing prey, show strong hostility toward strange wolves and battle like fury in defense of the young. Within their own circle they treat one another in the manner of friends and relatives. Pups are fondled by all the adults. The mother and the litter are provided with food and protected from danger.

Mech denies that the wolf is born with "a killer's instinct." He says instead that "it is born with certain be-

havior patterns that *allow it to learn to kill.*" The species is
adapted to eating fresh meat and can consume large quantities of it at a single meal. Given its strength, keenness,
intelligence and cooperative nature, the wolf is able to
hunt big game in the well-trained and organized pack.
Instead of being at each other's throats, the pack members
work efficiently at bringing down large prey animals that
they could not handle alone. The roving hunt is carried on
against a background of pack life that is highly organized
and complex.

"One day I watched a line of wolves heading along the
frozen shoreline of Isle Royale, in Lake Superior," Mech
recounted. "Suddenly they stopped and faced upwind toward a large moose. After a few seconds, the wolves as-
sembled closely, wagged their tails, and touched noses.
Then they started upwind single file toward the
moose . . ."

To Mech the incident demonstrated not only the order which exists within the wolf pack, but also the system of communication that makes close pack cooperation possible. They manage to keep in touch with each other during the night hunts. Wolves are capable of a wide range of vocal signals such as growls, whimpers, barks and howls. They use their lithe bodies to transmit numerous messages through postures and gestures. And their facial expressions communicate to each other a good deal of meaning.

Some of these signals indicate the relationships that exist within the pack at a given moment. Such activities as the hunt need both leaders and followers. Observers of free-living wolf packs have reported that some individuals appear dominant. Mech described wolf government as "a combination of autocratic and democratic systems."

"The leader usually seems to act independently of his packmates, with them dependent on him for direction.

However, he is influenced somewhat by the behavior of the other pack members." In traveling, hunting, feeding and mating, the so-called alpha male usually takes the initiative. But Mech and others have observed that, at times, another male may step into the leading role. Furthermore, leadership is by no means limited to males. Once they are freed from the daily care of the young, females may assume the dominant role. Although normally smaller than the male and lighter by about fifteen pounds, the female hunter is every bit as skilled and daring as the male. During the winter season, the wolf pack has been observed on the trail of prey, a female in the lead.

Students of animal behavior have sometimes assumed that dominance is essential to every mammal society and that the leadership "naturally" goes to the male of the species. The subject of dominance has drawn the keen interest of scientists looking at primates, those mammals that are "the closest kin of humankind."

9 · Apes and Their Kin

To learn how higher animals behave, avid seekers cross the time zones of the earth and the era boundaries of the ages. The curious find themselves at last in Africa.

Its deserts and rain forests, its savannas and uplands hold long-buried and presently living clues to the nature of higher animals. The African earth has given up rich fossil evidence about primates who preceded the human species. Here too abound the living apes and monkeys whose behavior sometimes appears like that of human-kind.

On a recent autumn evening, we sat nervously in a

halted Volkswagen on a dry plain in Zululand. Around us milled a large herd of wild Cape buffalo. Any one of these massive beasts might have rolled the little car over with the flick of a longhorn and left us as helpless as a bug on its back. We dared not try to move until the herd in its own time ambled on its dusty way.

The game reserve is strangely astir at this twilight moment. This is a crossroad in time, when the daylight species meet the awakening night prowlers. In the far distance, field glasses could be focused on grazing zebras, nimble springtailed warthogs, skittish and graceful hooved animals that may have been impalas or nyalas.

Our interest was centered, however, on a troop of chacma baboons, just within our range of vision in a small grove where they were settling down for the night. We had been tracking them throughout the day, able to catch only an occasional glimpse of their activities. Now, unfortunately, there was little to be seen at such a distance in the lowering dusk. The frustrating experience only heightened our appreciation of field research and the difficulties of the scientist who studies animals in native environments.

The habits of chacma baboons are still little known. These large, handsome, robust and perceptive animals may be seen in any good-sized zoological garden. But why is it necessary to journey to a remote part of the earth to see how this species lives? Do they really behave so uniquely in the African wilds?

At one time, those studying primates stood in two distinct and distant groups. There were those who insisted that field studies held all there was to be learned about these animals. Opposing this view were the experimental scientists working in the controlled conditions of the laboratory.

Both approaches are now understood to be necessary —

just as two eyes are needed for vision in depth. The lesson probably applies to the study of all animal species. But it holds especially true for the primates, who are in many ways almost as complex as human beings. They are highly social, sensitive to change, keenly intelligent and strongly emotional.

Who knows more about monkey behavior — the trained observer who lives with them in the wilderness or the lab researcher who watches them day after day through a one-way-vision mirror and then monitors them electronically through the nights? Neither scientist will claim to know it all. In fact, the more recent trend is for the student of animal behavior to divide time between observing free-living animals and those in captivity.

Peering at animals in the privacy of their native habitats does not satisfy all of our itching curiosities about them. Much primate research these days asks the question: How do animals learn? And lab experimentation has revealed a good deal about learning processes and teaching techniques.

Monkeys are astoundingly clever in getting at a bunch of bananas. They play an expert game of tick-tack-toe and unlatch a series of door locks in exactly the right order to reach members of the opposite sex. Most spectacular are the experiments in which chimpanzees seem to master sign language.

But the search for adaptive behavior that has survival value still turns us toward the wilderness. If we want to know how habits naturally occur and why animals act as they do, we need to go to the environment where these patterns evolved. In no other place can the behavior be truly and fully seen. Nowhere else does it have the same usefulness. When they are moved out of their native haunts, animals tend to leave their natural habits behind.

Most primates can adjust to some changes in living patterns. But they do not easily withstand the shock of exchanging the freedom of the wilds for captivity in a steel cage. Monkeys born in a research center's "maternity ward" are quite different from their cousins who begin life in the jungle. The placid temperament of a gorilla, suited to its life in a subtropical mountain environment, usually undergoes a complete change in the city zoo, where it may turn sullen, high-strung, vicious. The baboon separated from its troop is faced with unnatural conditions which affect its behavior. Once a social animal like an ape finds itself living alone, it is no longer the same. As one veteran observer of primates put it, "One chimpanzee is not a chimpanzee at all."

Any disruption of orderly and natural group patterns of living has a profound effect on all types of primate behavior. What probably suffers most of all is the normal conduct between males and females. Many animals are totally unable to reproduce their young in captivity. Caged animals who are isolated or cut off from their normal associations and environments may suffer extreme shock, become fearful and withdrawn, lose their curiosity and interest in their new environment, the objects or animals in it.

Repeatedly, scientists studying animal behavior have been misled by theories based entirely on the observation of captive animals. It may be useful to report how members of a species act under certain artificial conditions. But this cannot become an accurate general statement about the natural behavior of the species. It is now clear that the aggression of animals is heightened when they are frustrated by captivity. They may become very competitive when their food supply is controlled by human captors.

Even more troublesome to students of animal behavior are the changes that take place when research teams move out into the wilderness. It is now recognized that the slightest human interference in the wild environments of higher animals may deeply affect their natural behavior.

In the early 1960s, when primate research was beginning to expand at a great rate, a young British woman ventured alone into the thickly forested uplands that border East Africa's Lake Tanganyika. This was Jane Goodall, who has since married and become Jane Van Lawick-Goodall.

She had a clear notion of what she wanted to find out — nothing less than the natural habits of wild chimpanzees, living as they have for centuries in the unspoiled forested valley of the Gombe Stream. Goodall managed to complete a research program of high scientific value. But she did not succeed altogether in keeping the wild habitat unchanged. She changed it herself — by her very coming.

By the third year of her African primate study, Jane Goodall settled into an easy relationship with the large company of chimpanzees whom she observed daily. In order to identify them clearly in her own mind, she had given a name to each of the males and females, the young and the adults. Although chimpanzee communities are not ruled by a single supreme overlord, Goodall had always considered the robust and easygoing Goliath as the No. 1 male. However, the center of the stage was soon to be taken by Mike, a morose younger male, a kind of lone outsider.

Chimps are normally noisy. But neither the apes nor the human beings in the Gombe Stream Reserve were prepared for Mike's noisemaking talents. Mike had often toyed with some of the four-gallon kerosine cans lying about the camp. And he had learned what deafening and awesome sounds could be made by hurling them, bouncing them on rocks or banging two of them together. On one autumn morning, Goodall watched with growing excitement as Mike began what was to become a bold thrust for power. The chimpanzee called attention to himself by a display of rising fury. Brandishing two empty kerosine cans, Mike stood swaying from side to side, hooting and panting, his rocking movements gradually becoming wilder and more fearsome. The chimpanzee colony watched in silence.

Suddenly, Mike lunged through the gathering of males, bouncing his cans and crashing off into the forest. At once he was back, this time making straight for Goliath. The leader retreated. And in the next moments, the other males crowded around Mike, making friendly and appeasing gestures.

Thus Goodall recorded "the spectacular rise of a male named Mike to the top-ranking position in the community." The old leader, Goliath, later made a few attempts at regaining his position. But he too finally crouched and cowered before the new leader. At no time in the contest was there any real violence or bloodshed. Mike had won by means of threat and bluff — and empty kerosine cans.

Was Mike a "born leader" who would inevitably have found his way to the top position? Or had human beings, altering the wild environment, prompted this conflict, unwittingly putting into Mike's hands the instruments of power? Questions of this kind troubled Jane Goodall from the moment she became an inhabitant of the African wilds.

She was only twenty-four when this slight, attractive blond British woman first appeared in east Africa. She had come to work with the famous anthropologist, L. S. B. Leakey, who was soon to discover, in the Olduvai Gorge, the remains of apelike human ancestors.

It was during this period that Jane Goodall expressed interest in the behavior of primates who had preceded humankind. And it was Dr. Leakey who stirred Goodall's hopes of learning something about prehuman behavior through the study of modern free-living apes.

In 1960, Goodall arrived in what is now western Tanzania, eager to learn about the behavior of chimpanzees.

A common gesture is what the scientists call "presenting" — turning the backside toward another animal. At times, this is done by the female in heat offering her hindquarters to an adult male. However, much of what is called presenting is merely a display by which one animal greets or gives way to another. It is a kind of salute that seems to express, "At your service." Usually, the act has no direct sexual significance. It may involve two males or two females, or juveniles not mature enough for mating.

One kind of intimate activity in which all chimps spend a great deal of time is called "social grooming." This is a friendly form of close physical contact, clearly enjoyed by all. Jane Goodall cited an incident in which an elderly chimp with paralyzed legs painfully dragged himself sixty yards to be in a circle of grooming males.

Goodall became engrossed in the play activities of the chimpanzees, a type of behavior common to all primate species. Much of this is rough-and-tumble — climbing, chasing, sham battles, tickling, show-off stunts, throwing things, free and vigorous romping that seems to express nothing but high spirits and sheer joy in movement. In its mocking antics, its mischievous grinning and make-believe facial expressions, the ape at play comes closest to being like ourselves. "Even when watching the wildest games," wrote Goodall, "I seldom heard a sound unless I was close enough to hear the soft panting that is the equivalent of human laughter."

She made a keen study of chimpanzee play, discovering its many uses. For the growing youngster, this is a pleasant way of learning about its natural and social environment for living in it as an adult. Noted Goodall: "Social play certainly offers the young chimp the opportunity to become familiar with other youngsters." In their play, primate juveniles make awkward mounting attempts long before they are capable of reproductive activity. Some of this is exploratory sex play, imitating the adult behaviors of court-

ship and mating. Research has shown that such play experience and practice is necessary if the young are to
become adults fully capable of mating.

As she observed social behaviors, Jane Goodall became
increasingly aware that her small research station was affecting not only the "wildness" of the natural environment
but also the behavior of the chimpanzee community. She
realized that her first two years would remain her "good
old days" at the Gombe Stream Reserve. During that
period it had still been possible to make authentic studies
of natural chimpanzee behavior. However, once the
chimps were tamed and touched by human visitors, drawn
to the base camp and its free food, the animals were never
quite themselves again. She knew that her first big mistake
came when she handed a chimpanzee a banana for the first
time. "I realize now that you must not get too familiar with
these wild animals," she said. She had learned a costly
lesson.

Goodall was wary from the first of another hindrance to
animal behavior research — the prejudice of the observer,
who may prejudge what is to be observed and decide in
advance what kinds of behavior are most important. "The
only sure way of finding out how animals really live and
behave is to watch them for long periods of time — and
watch them without fixed ideas about what they are
doing," Goodall wrote. "Unfortunately, many scientists set
out to prove a preconceived theory."

Jane Goodall learned from her research in the wilds the
significance of peaceful, friendly social relationships in a
chimpanzee community. Other observers seem to attach
greater importance to conflict, male supremacy and the
struggle for power.

"Alpha" is the name often given by scientists to the one
ape or monkey considered to be "dominant" in a studied

group. In rank order, the rest of the animals are named with the succeeding letters of the Greek alphabet.

Unfortunately, the matter of "Who's who?" in a chimpanzee band or a baboon troop is rarely that fixed or simple. Recent studies of nonhuman primates have cast doubt on such rigid ideas about dominance and hierarchies.

Primate research, enormously expanded in the last decade, now shows that the species vary greatly in their social behavior. Studies of animals in the wild state reveal that there is no one common pattern that will describe the social organizations of Japanese macaques, mid-African baboons, South American howler monkeys and Indian langurs. As for the apes — gorillas, gibbons, orangutans and chimps — they differ widely in the size of groups, the nature of family life, the types of leadership and the relationships between males and females.

Among the hamadryas baboons of arid northeast Africa, small family groups, which include several adult females, are each clearly controlled by a single male. But among the wild patas monkeys of the African grasslands it is often the females who take charge of safeguarding the group against danger. In gorilla society, "alpha" is boss. On the other hand, Jane Goodall observed that chimpanzees have "a loose social order, with temporary groups, no sexual jealousies, no permanent leaders, and little fighting or aggressive behavior."

"Dominance" may have many meanings — or none at all. One individual in a monkey group may be its most active defender and not be masterful in any other way. In a baboon troop on the march, it is the "lower-ranking" younger males who usually take the lead. Among gibbons, both sexes share in leading, unifying and guarding the group.

Monkeys and apes in the wild show little tendency to defend territories. They do not ordinarily "stand and fight" against enemies. In case of a major threat, the entire company escapes. So-called dominant males are often seen running faster than anyone else. They offer little help to the mothers carrying young, who usually bring up the rear.

At times, some members of a primate group may perform a "police" role, keeping order, suppressing quarrels. A strong individual may carry out this function without the use of force, by means of an angry growl, a threatening stare, or merely a yawn that displays a set of sharp teeth. Even though males are more robust in most species, females also act as peacekeepers.

Leaders of primate groups do not rely entirely on brute strength and fighting ability. Mastery is sometimes won by sheer bluff. But more often, the leader is the one who has the best relationships within the entire group and can win the support of a kind of leading council. Intelligence and experience are factors in the making of a leader, who is sometimes an elderly member of the group.

The forming of a hierarchy can often be seen as an adaptive response to scarcity of food, or danger from predators, to overcrowding or stress. Many reports of dominance among primates were based largely on studies of animals in captivity. On the typical zoo "monkey island," life in captivity has usually brought about a strict, military kind of hierarchy in which each animal knows his or her "place."

Under such circumstances, a single supreme male "alpha" may become overlord. He may seize the best and the most food, occupy the choice site for resting and sunning, and take his pick of the females for mating.

Scientists have often measured dominance in the laboratory by throwing out bits of food among crowds of hungry animals and recording which ones win out in the intense rivalry. Under experimental conditions, it is possible to bring about a ferocious struggle for power. Often animals act more "wild" in captivity than they do in the wilderness! Free-living baboons observed by one scientist in Uganda, Africa, were not governed by a strong system of leadership. However, when she studied this same species in a caged area, all the males and females were arrayed in a strict hierarchy, the top places won through fierce competition.

It has been tempting for many observers to look at primates in terms of human society, since these are the animals who are most like ourselves. Monkeys and apes seen through the bars of a cage appear to mirror human behavior. And even highly trained scientists have been misled into assuming that male dominance is "natural" to all primates. After all, these scientists do themselves live in societies in which the slogan "ladies first" applies only to the most trivial matters and males ordinarily run the government, the economy, the military and largely control the social structure. How easy it is to interpret the male role in primate society in these terms — and to assume that a female can only reach a higher status if she is chosen by a high-ranking male!

While many of the early scientific observers of primates have been fascinated by dominance and competition, fighting and aggressiveness, others now attach at least equal importance to other phases of the social behavior of these animals. Among the primates are to be seen remarkable examples of animal communication, playfulness, curiosity, learning and teaching ability. They also come closest to human beings in expressing affection.

As among most mammals, the closest relationships are to be seen between mother and child. However, in many primate species, the males also care for the young. Among the small monkeys of South America, the fathers transport the infants most of the time, only handing them over to the mothers for breast-feeding.

Adult male baboons show a lively interest in infants; in fact, the most powerful leaders of the troops allow the young to clamber all over them and to maul them playfully in ways that no other adult would dare. Studies of monkeys in Japan reveal that the males take full charge of the young during the time when the females are giving birth and nursing new offspring. In recent experimental research at the University of California, male rhesus monkeys showed themselves fully willing and able to raise orphaned juveniles.

Monkeys and apes are in the habit of grooming one another. This takes more time than any other activity. Grooming is a way in which primates care for one another, probably reducing the tensions of everyday life in the wilderness and soothing the frustrations of animals in captivity. Primates express their concern for one another by this kind of gentle touching that covers every part of the body.

No one can even guess at the feelings of an animal while it is being groomed. What the observer sees is that the groomed monkey or ape appears relaxed and placid. The animal may lie stretched full length, its eyes half-closed, breathing slowly, responding to the soothing, caressing movements of its partner. Grooming seems to express friendliness and goodwill, strengthening the bonds between the members of a primate group. Throughout this activity, there is constant lip-smacking and soft murmuring. The two partners take turns, seeming to enjoy both grooming and being groomed.

In their natural habitats, primates are observed grooming at several times during the day — at the time of rising from sleep, during a quiet midday period and at dusk just before bedtime. Mutual grooming is joined in freely by individuals of all levels and ranks and ages in a primate society. It is by no means only a sexual or courting activity, even though it does play a big part in the relationships between males and females.

The term "grooming" hardly begins to describe the real

importance of this social behavior. The grooming pairs do cleanse each other. They comb through the fur with their fingers, picking off burrs and ticks, seeds and grit.

But is all this just a matter of tidiness? An answer may be found by comparing animals in the wilds and under laboratory conditions. Do monkeys groom each other in a primate research center, where they are living under the most sanitary conditions? Grooming goes on there just as actively as in the wilderness of northern India.

Half a world away from the native home of rhesus monkeys is a huge caged colony of them in Madison, Wisconsin. We spent some time there recently in a set of three low buildings just off the state university campus. We were saying farewell there to the retiring longtime director of the Primate Research Center, Dr. Harry F. Harlow.

He recalled how a small towel, accidentally left in the cage of a young monkey, had led almost twenty years ago to a set of experiments which have since become world-famous. The monkey was one of sixty which had been raised in complete isolation from their mothers and all other monkeys. The manner in which this rhesus clung frantically to the towel started Harlow testing the emotional needs of these small primates. The desperate urge of the monkey to clutch what Harlow called a "cloth mother" proved to be even stronger than its desire for food. As Harlow put it, "Body contact was of overpowering importance."

Some of us will ask: Why? How can this clinging habit be explained? Or, to put the query differently: Is there any way in which this behavior is adaptive, linked to species survival?

The question may not find any complete answer in the campus laboratory. But perhaps it does sound an echo in some distant wilderness where monkeys and apes are at home. Natural selection is a process by which animals are adapted to their own environments. In the wild it is evident that the primate baby who does not cling — will probably not survive!

The monkey infant, born helpless, develops slowly and spends its early years in strong dependency on adults. It is breast-fed, and it is nourished solely on a diet of mother's milk for an extended period. Primate mothers are devoted, patient, easygoing and slow to wean their babies from suckling to adult foods.

There is much more than food, however, that the primate baby gets at its mother's bosom. The young one vitally needs to be touched and gently stroked. While nestled against the maternal bosom, the infant is protected, comforted, warmed, nurtured, caressed. Only with a deep sense of well-being can the primate baby grow to normal adulthood.

Throughout this early period, the infant does not break contact with its mother, never letting go for even an instant. Meanwhile, the mother must be active — foraging for food, escaping from danger, traveling constantly with the group since social life is necessary for survival. While the parent goes about her business, the infant literally hangs on for life. It grasps the mother's hair and skin with fingers and toes. Some monkeys — baboons, langurs and rhesus — also get a firm grip on the mother's nipple with their teeth.

Among some species of animals, parents transport their young by mouth. But active primate life hardly allows for such a method. Moreover, primate hands and feet are highly developed for grasping. Even though many apes and some monkeys have long ago abandoned the trees, all have special adaptations to tree-living.

The grip of the brown langur infant on its mother's body is so tight that the two can swing rapidly through the treetops at astonishing speeds, without pause. The gibbon mother feeds at the ends of long branches swaying in the high winds. Perilously, it dangles there briefly before it plunges to a lower branch or leaps across yawning space. Throughout these aerial flights, the baby remains firmly attached.

The primate mother's body offers a hundred protections. It is shelter against rainstorms and high winds, a refuge against untold parasites, injuries, diseases. Until the offspring is better able to move by itself across rocky terrain or to travel aloft through the network of trees, its safest place is at its mother's breast.

The young animal that does not learn to cling properly is a menace to itself, to its parent and to the entire social group. Once it lets go, the infant may be instantly seized by a stalking leopard or a soaring hawk. A mother hampered by a loose infant is in peril. And the entire primate community may be slowed in its search for food or escape from enemies. In many ways, the clinging behavior of primate infants is a matter of life and death.

How much of what we see in such animal habits can be directly applied to human beings? Is the monkey offspring, clinging to the hair of a female parent, performing the same behavior as the human infant curled at its mother's breast? And are both kinds of mothers — and mothers in general — all linked together by an unbroken chain of maternal behavior?

And what of the human male? Is he doomed by his genes to be forever a kind of imitation gorilla, thumping his chest in a show of rage to prove he is dominant and superior and male? And is he destined by nature to be a stranger to his own offspring, as are the fathers of some apes and monkeys?

These are perplexing kinds of questions that students of behavior face. They are problems for all of us as well — since the answers may have a lot to do with how we conduct our lives.

10·Human...and Unique

"Man and all the other vertebrate animals have been constructed on the same general model," wrote Charles Darwin. "All the bones in his skeleton can be compared with the corresponding bones in monkey, bat or seal."

In revealing the biological oneness of all living forms, Darwin affirmed that humankind was descended from extinct primates and had evolved as a distinct species. But while the origins of human bodily structure were clear a century ago, the workings of human behavior were not. And even if there are some similarities in outward appearance, the behaviors of humans and other animal species have little in common.

The human being is unique in conduct. There is a brain at work here that sets this species apart. The special human quality produces logic and planning, language and education, science and art. No other animal has the peculiar human powers to create and to love, to act by whim or will. Equipped with such a mind, the human being is able to break free from the dominance of inborn behavioral patterns.

This species is social. But its sociality is not that of the beehive, fish school, bird flock, wolf pack. Human beings, alone among animals, are the builders of cultures — complex, evolving forms that provide a framework for human behavior and a means of transmitting learned behavior from generation to generation.

However, with all humankind's self-awareness and ability to reason, people are still their own greatest mystery. The species is wrapped in riddles. We see only dimly through a mist of confusion and complexity. Are answers to the big human questions to be found mainly in turning backward toward the animal world? Are our behaviors, like our bones, traceable to "monkey, bat or seal"? Or do the solutions lie in that peculiar mode of human development — culture?

In Darwin's time, there was nothing like today's probing into the ways in which societies, human and animal, function. Neither Darwin nor any other scientist of his day had made any significant scientific studies of human behavior. There was no science of genetics; the action of hormones was unknown; the study of psychology was in its infancy, the science of anthropology not yet born. Human behavior was still shrouded in the mystery of "instincts." Behaviors accepted as "proper" by a given culture were seen as fixed by "human nature." Still unasked were many questions about the wide varieties of human living patterns that have emerged in every age and throughout the habitable places of this planet.

Darwin was himself a product of one distinctive way of life known as "Victorianism." The Victorian era, named after Queen Victoria of England, was a tumultuous period of social change that affected not only England but much of Europe and America as well. Cities and industries were growing at a rapid pace. Millions were migrating to urban and factory centers from the countryside, thus changing longtime habits. This was a business-minded era that put a high value on "success" and raised the competitive spirit to new heights. Aggressive rivalries mounted between the great powers vying for world markets and colonial empires. Within the major nations these same "go-getter" attitudes prevailed at home.

The period saw the spectacular rise of the middle class. Members of this segment of society not only pushed themselves to power and prominence in business and government. They also developed rigid codes of conduct, including ideals of male and female behavior which have been approved in Western society up to the present day.

The manners and morality of the age called for prudish conduct in dress and in language and etiquette pertaining to male-female relationships. The model man of the Victorian period was aggressive, shrewd, self-reliant and venturesome. More than ever the male appeared as sole provider and head of the household. The ideal middle-class woman was chaste in thought and deed, obedient to her husband, a devoted wife and mother. Society did not approve of careers for women outside the home. Homemaking and child-rearing were even more firmly fixed as the lifelong female role. A woman's status in the larger society was a reflection of that of her mate.

By the early decades of this century, there were stirrings of female revolt, climaxed in the successful struggle of women to win the vote. New developments in the biological and social sciences also raised doubts about the Victorian code of female subservience and male dominance. Some women suggested that perhaps this arrangement was no more "natural" or "God-given" than was chattel slavery or the divine right of kings!

By the early years of this century, scientists had begun in earnest to investigate the ways in which social behavior develops, raising a good many new questions about "human nature." Does every human society have its own patterns of conduct? Then perhaps it is the societies themselves that will reveal why people behave as they do.

It was this kind of thinking that led social scientists like Margaret Mead into the remote human habitats of the earth. In the 1920s, this bold young American woman ventured among the peoples of the South Pacific islands. Much of her research would later be summarized in a book to be called *Male and Female*.

In October, 1925, Margaret Mead landed in Samoa to begin the first of her superb field studies of tribal peoples. The islanders revealed themselves to the gentle probing and the keen observing of this twenty-three-year-old anthropologist. Speaking their language, eating their food, sitting barefoot and cross-legged on the pebbly coral floor of a thatched dwelling, she began to trace out the patterns of social behavior.

Over the next quarter century, she would study intently seven different South Pacific societies, comparing theirs with American life-styles, weaving the design of "the sexes in a changing world." Sex roles were colored threads running throughout her writing as she portrayed the intricate ways in which males and females relate to each other.

The daughter of a Pennsylvania professor, Margaret Mead had spent her growing-up years in the company of scholars. Early in her own rich education, she chose a career in the rapidly changing field of anthropology, particularly in the study of human cultures. To understand her own species, she felt she had to know the outer limits of its social behavior. Only through field studies could she learn firsthand some of the varied ways in which humankind lives.

The science of anthropology has outgrown the notion that peoples outside the mainstreams of the major civilizations are remnants of earlier forms of human existence, living now as our ancestors did. The anthropologist does not study these societies to find the sources of how Europeans or Americans behave.

These are ways of life that may be immensely different from ours. In Polynesia and along the Arctic Circle, in central Africa and among the Indians of both American continents, there are societies as old and stable as our own. These peoples have developed cultures that express their own needs and throw light on the capability of human beings to act in ways that suit themselves.

In Samoa, Mead fell in with a placid tempo of village life that was pleasant and harmonious. Children were early introduced to what the society regarded as proper behavior for boys and girls. Throughout their childhood, the girls were involved in baby tending. In time, they learned to weave fibers, to fish from the reef and to cook, to prepare themselves for marriage and duties as wives. The boys were trained as house builders, fishermen, orators, woodcarvers.

In this society, title and rank were important. As Mead pointed out, "A wife's rank can never exceed her husband's because it is always directly dependent on it."

The Samoans, she found, were a genial, pleasure-loving

NEW GUINEA

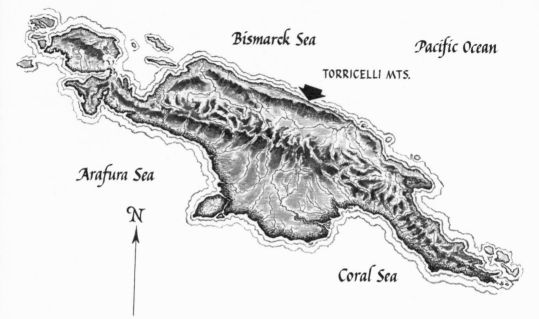

Bismarck Sea

Pacific Ocean

TORRICELLI MTS.

Arafura Sea

N

Coral Sea

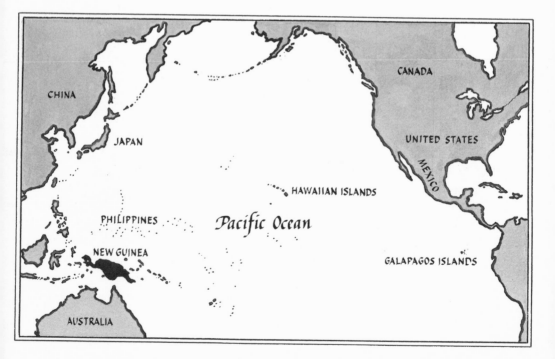

CHINA

JAPAN

PHILIPPINES

NEW GUINEA

AUSTRALIA

CANADA

UNITED STATES

MEXICO

HAWAIIAN ISLANDS

Pacific Ocean

GALAPAGOS ISLANDS

people. Both women and men enjoyed their own sexuality, keeping their free behavior within the bounds of well-established if unwritten codes.

To New Guinea, Margaret Mead came in 1931 with her deep interest in the different ways in which cultures defined the roles of males and females, setting patterns of behavior that were approved and expected. The series of studies that began with the Arapesh were to bring her some new insights into the nature of sex roles.

Living poorly on an unfertile mountain, the Arapesh society did not prompt the two sexes to sharply differentiated behavior. In spite of the harsh conditions of their lives, these people were gentle and generous, trusting and kindly toward each other. The description equally fitted both the men and the women.

Very early in life, each little Arapesh girl became pledged to a somewhat older boy. During long years of betrothal, the male was more like a father or older brother than he was like a suitor. The girl lived in the home of her in-laws until her young husband was ready to provide a dwelling for the two of them.

Their children would be equally nurtured by both of the parents, treated with tenderness and care. The parents would share in providing food and other needs. If a husband died, his wife and her children would expect to move into the home of her brother-in-law. She might then become a second wife. Such customs had been handed down through countless generations of the Arapesh.

In what she described as the orderly pattern and texture of village life, Mead recorded "the quiet uneventful cooperation, singing in the cold dawn and singing and laughter in the evening, men who sit happily playing to themselves on hand-drums, women holding suckling children to their breasts, young girls walking easily down the center of the village, with the walk of those who are cherished by all about them."

Occasionally, the calmness of the village routine might be shattered by angriness and dispute, by unfairness and the charge that sorcery was being used by one person against another. But these disruptions were rare and short-lived. Arapesh society did not approve of such behavior. And to Margaret Mead, it was now becoming clear in what ways a society evokes the kinds of behavior it approves.

As the Arapesh were mild and trusting, so the Mundugumor tribesmen on the turbulent Yuat River were bad-tempered and suspicious. From childhood on, these New Guinea people grew up hostile and violent, insecure and aggressive.

To Margaret Mead the contrast with the Arapesh could hardly have been greater. It was almost unbelievable that this same island would produce peoples with behaviors so different from each other.

She lived among the Mundugumor in much discomfort, distressed by the lack of human warmth, the arrogance, the strange kind of joy these people took in their own violent behavior. The women occupied themselves individually at gardening and fishing, the men in raids on enemy tribes and warlike ceremonials.

As Margaret Mead explored more deeply the life patterns of New Guinea societies, she discovered that the entire island was a kind of showcase in the different ways men and women live with each other.

Although the Arapesh and Mundugumor societies were strikingly different from each other, neither set contrasting standards for male and female behavior. It was the Tchambuli people who displayed quite another social picture. In fact, to Margaret Mead, this was the "missing piece" in a study of contrasts. The Tchambuli were a small tribe living at the edge of a placid black-water lake and in the shadow of a mountain. In this society, the women held the positions of real power. Efficient, brisk, hearty, they managed the business of the community, working cooperatively in large female groups. These women shaved their heads and didn't bother trying to beautify themselves. They had no time for quarreling, loafing, gossiping. These were male activities!

Mead found the men absorbed in artistic interests. They were skilled in dancing, carving, mask-making, flute-playing. Their days were spent in preparing elaborate ceremonials and entertainments which were highly praised by the women.

In this society, the women chose their mates. And the young men lived in a nervous state of anxiety, fearing they would not be well chosen by the females who were the best breadwinners.

"It was the girls who were bright and free," wrote Margaret Mead, "while the small boys were already caught up in the rivalrous, catty, and individually competitive life of the men."

The Tchambuli village was a far cry from the male-dominated American society in which Margaret Mead had grown up. It was something like Philadelphia — but in reverse!

"Personality traits which we have called masculine or feminine," Margaret Mead concluded, "are as lightly linked to sex as are the clothing, the manners, and the form of head-dress that a society at a given period assigns to either sex."

The search for the sources of human behavior seems to point us toward the special ways in which human societies develop, the process called "cultural evolution."

Every human society probably includes the full range of personal differences. But a society selects only a few temperaments, habits and behaviors which are considered "proper" for each sex. These approved behaviors are upheld, praised, rewarded by the society. Contrary behaviors are discouraged or punished.

In this fashion, each society seems to invent and maintain its own models of male and female conduct. Such stereotypes are embedded in every culture. Typically, each culture is loyal to its own particular stereotypes. The tendency is to believe they are the "true" ones. But behavior that is highly approved in one culture may be taboo in the next. And very likely no two societies would agree on a checklist of approved male and female behavior.

Every society has cast males and females into typical roles. But the actors themselves may have some troublesome questions. Is it our physical makeup that decides how we are to perform? Are we somehow destined by our anatomy to play out these parts?

In a story often told, a little girl was visiting an art museum with her grandmother, pausing before a painting which depicted the biblical first couple in the Garden of Eden.

"Yes, I know who they are," whispered the girl, perplexed, "but who is who?"

"You mean you can't tell which is Adam and which is Eve?" asked the grandmother.

"No," came the reply. "They haven't any clothes on!"

Believable or not, the story illustrates a characteristic of human beings. Males and females are not as differentiated as they are in a great many other species. In the animal world, the two sexes may be unlike in size and shape, color and smell, in sounds and gestures, in fighting equipment, muscularity, scales, feathers and fur. As we have seen, the female spider is many times larger than the male. Peacock and rooster, ram and gander, bull moose and he-lion are all males easily distinguished from the females of their kind.

Among human males and females, there are some apparent biological differences in addition to those in the sexual organs and their functions. Men tend to be somewhat larger and have deeper voices. Women tend to develop earlier in their sexual maturity, in reaching adult height, in the growth of bones and teeth. Men usually have more face and body hair, but are prone to baldness. A woman is generally wider in hip dimensions than a male of the same height and similar bone structure, the female pelvis being shaped somewhat differently from that of the male. Such statements are based on statistical averages, but they say little about the countless humans, male and female, who do not conform to these generalizations. Nor do the figures tell us anything about important qualities that cannot be so easily measured.

What do we know about any innate differences in the mentality and abilities of the two sexes? Human cultures through the ages have built systems of belief around the differing reproductive functions of the sexes. These beliefs have extended into every phase of life. Males and females have been depicted as different in nature and therefore destined to play separate social roles. Yet for all the scientific measuring and testing that has gone on, especially in the last two decades, little has been proved about natural differences between the two sexes. Indeed, as individuals, both sexes seem to display the full rainbow spectrum of human temperaments, mentalities, behaviors, abilities.

To some extent, physical differences between males and females have in the past provided some basis for a social division of labor between them. Since women bear and suckle babies, they have mainly been responsible for childcare in many societies. In simpler cultures, where hunting is common, men have tended to be more active in duties related to supplying food.

However, the new realities of life today have lessened any basis for a division of labor according to sex. Modern trends in work show less need for heavy, unskilled and field labor and more jobs available in skilled factory and office work, civil service, social work, and the professions. More than ever, women are finding socially useful careers in such employment — in any society that grants women equal opportunities with men. The growing experience of many nations is that jobs once performed primarily by men are now being done just as capably by women.

Though it is still widely believed, as it was in the Victorian era, that homemaking is *the* proper female occupation, a woman's potentialities are today less than ever limited to the tasks of bearing and raising children. The trend is toward smaller families in a world already heavily overpopulated, and family planning is practiced by millions. On the average, today's woman spends a small segment of her life span bound to the responsibilities of maternity.

Even in simple agricultural societies where women do hard work, they ordinarily pause only a few short weeks for the birth of a child and soon return to the fields. In industrialized countries, maternity has long been used as a basis for discrimination against women employees. The bias against women results from the notion that women alone are responsible for children. The child also belongs to the father, but somehow his parenthood is not seen as affecting his work.

Thus mothers are deprived of careers outside the home, and fathers of the joys of child-raising. The sexist society that discriminates against women loses the full potentialities of all its members and denies its people the full pleasures of life.

Margaret Mead observed that the society which severely limits the behavior of the two sexes is wasteful of the natural gifts of both men and women. "Where one sex suffers, the other suffers also," declared this clear-minded social scientist, who had grown wise studying the cultures of the world. "We need every human gift, and we cannot turn down any human offering because of race, class, natural origin or sex."

At an early age, children ordinarily become aware that they are either male or female. Most experts in child development agree that this kind of self-identity is extremely important for healthy growth. The child, they say, should have a definite sense of being a member of either one sex or the other.

There are rare cases on record of children born with physical defects so that they are not clearly linked with either sex. However, most problems of sexual identity seem to have little to do with physical traits. The confusion may be more directly linked to the particular society — and whatever it has selected as "normal" behavior.

When a society defines male or female conduct too narrowly, many of its members may have trouble knowing or accepting where they are supposed to belong. If approved male behavior is described as aggressive, goal-driven, insensitive, competitive, then some males will be unwilling to conform. If the society says that females must be passive, fearful, docile, subservient — some will accept this role, but others will rebel. Some members of both sexes will be unable to conform and may lead unhappy, anxious lives trying to be something which they are not. Members of neither sex are being allowed by the society to be fully themselves.

Every social order does need certain rules and guidelines for the behavior of its members. But sometimes such a code is an outmoded holdover from the past and no longer useful. It may in fact stand in the way of a society which is trying to move toward an improved way of life for its members.

Most troublesome of all seems to be a social dogma that tells either sex that it is better, more important or more valuable than the other.

Anthropologists have noted as a general pattern that males tend to assert their own importance throughout human societies. It is not at all clear why most men seem to need a sense of superiority. Some observers have suggested that since they do not go through the mother's experience in childbirth, males may be unsure about their own parental role and may seek a sense of importance to reassure themselves. Whatever the reason, the male occupation is often given a higher value by a society.

"Men may cook, or weave or dress dolls or hunt humming birds," Mead pointed out, "but if such activities are appropriate activities of men, then the whole society votes them as important."

It may seem difficult to deny that the bearing and raising of children are among the most creative of all human acts. And yet, male-ruled societies commonly belittle these activities. Among the Manus people on a southwest Pacific island, Margaret Mead found the women deeply dissatisfied because the role of wife and mother is held in such low esteem. This pattern is seen in many societies in which women hold a subordinate place. In such societies, females live under the burden of being considered inferior.

However, men are not necessarily content with the roles chosen for them by their society — even when their sex holds power. The position of mastery seems to have its own discomforts and drawbacks, for the males are expected to live up to their "superiority" and prove their manhood.

Yet many men and women have no desire for a "battle of the sexes," nor that there be either victor or victim, a "superior" or "inferior" sex. Evidently human societies are still groping with the problems of forming a suitable framework for social behavior.

What are men and women? They are human beings from first to last, all sharing the characteristics of the species. That they are members of two distinct sexes is a biological fact of life. But if one sex is labeled inferior, that has nothing to do with biology.

How is such an opinion upheld? There are still many people in the world who quote some kind of holy writ to "prove" the inferiority of women. Others have packaged this same dogma in scientific wrappings. They claim that women have evolved as inferior beings and that the lower status of women is a biological inevitability.

Some of those bent on keeping women "in their place" take the view that human behavior is largely innate and instinctual. They see sexual roles as a part of human destiny, inherited through the genes and beyond the control of human will. In spite of the strong scientific evidence that human behavior is not controlled by instincts, such beliefs keep returning in new forms.

Still another argument for the supremacy of males also points toward the past, to human origins in lower forms of life. The suggestion is sometimes made that we are bound by natural laws to carry out the behavior patterns of our animal ancestors. This notion is hardly scientific.

Although the theory of natural selection says no such thing, Charles Darwin has sometimes been accused unjustly of "making a monkey out of man." Actually, the real attempt to deny human beings their humanness has very ancient origins.

A myth whispered throughout the ages and retold in many cultures is that the human being is nothing more than "a two-legged beast," "a mere animal," "a plumeless biped," "a hairless ape."

In recent years, some writers on the human species have almost succeeded in turning us back toward a dark age. A popular trend is to stress the "animal nature" of human beings. The human species is pictured as being full of murky greeds, aggressive passions and hunger for power, supposedly inherited from ravenous and brutal ancestors. We are pictured as thinly disguised brutes who are the slaves of our own deep, dark "animal nature," driven by wild, bestial instincts we can never fully understand or overcome.

In the lowest forms of life, free choice of behavior is indeed limited. However, human beings are not insects crawling on the earth or wild creatures limited to a blind, fierce struggle to exist, doomed to conduct beyond our control. The behavior of our species depends strongly on learning, reason and will. Distinct from lower animals, humankind can take a hand in its own destiny. We are highly capable of change. Culture, the decisive force in continuing human development, has moved us toward knowing ourselves, and solving our problems.

As males and females, we are not merely breeders, perpetuating the species. We can express our sexuality in caring and creative ways, relating deeply to one another, sharing the enjoyment of some of life's greatest pleasures. Human parenthood becomes not a matter of animal impulses but of responsible choices.

We know at last how fully our male and female behavior is of our own making. That knowledge reveals our own power for change, for adapting our behavior to our own deepest needs. Can we free ourselves from self-made rules that reduce the social worth and the self-esteem of members of both sexes?

Margaret Mead sees our new insights into human sexuality as among the most useful discoveries of our age. With them, she believes, it is now possible for men and women to shape "a more flexible, more varied society than the human race has ever built."

In human behavior, the deepest mysteries remain. We have only begun to know the inner stirrings of our hearts and minds, the spurs that move us to act. But somehow we are not quite the same fearful wanderers as were the first human newcomers on the earth.

We have come a long way from the wilderness, and our animal past. Ahead, there is nothing but freedom to behave as we choose, wisely or not.

Suggestions for Further Reading

Alland, Alexander, Jr. *The Human Imperative.* New York: Columbia University Press, 1972.
> Here is an anthropologist's view of the factors that underlie the behavior of human beings.

Carson, Rachel. *The Edge of the Sea.* Boston: Houghton Mifflin Co., 1955.
> An able scientist uses her matchless writing skills to describe animal behavior on the land-sea border and reproductive patterns in a changeful environment.

Dubos, Rene. *Beast or Angel?* New York: Charles Scribner's Sons, 1974.
> In examining "the choices that make us human," this biologist discusses the path of development that humankind has taken since diverging from other species.

Fabre, J. Henri. *The Life of Spiders.* New York: Horizon Press, 1971.
> An acute observer of animal behavior describes his adventures in the spider world.

Mead, Margaret. *Sex and Temperament in Three Primitive Societies.* New York: William Morrow and Co., 1963.
> Living among tribal peoples, an American anthropologist reveals how the behaviors of males and females are conditioned by the attitudes of the society in which they live.

Mech, David L. *The Wolf: The Ecology and Behavior of an Endangered Species*. Garden City: Natural History Press, 1970.
> Based on studies in the wild, this book separates facts from fantasies about one of the most misunderstood of all animals, the wolf.

Michelmore, Susan. *Sexual Reproduction*. Garden City: Natural History Press, 1970.
> This is a useful book that explains in clear fashion the essential features of the two-sex process of reproducing young.

Tinbergen, Niko, and the Editors of Time-Life. *Animal Behavior*. New York: Time-Life Books, 1965.
> One of the pioneers in the new science of ethology has put together a dramatic, well-illustrated and very readable account of his own research and that of fellow scientists.

Van Lawick-Goodall, Jane. *In the Shadow of Man*. Boston: Houghton Mifflin Co., 1971.
> This author's study of wild chimpanzees, one of the species most closely related to humankind, serves to point up the unique quality of human behavior.

von Frisch, Karl. *Man and the Living World*. New York: Harcourt Brace Jovanovich, 1963.
> In this easily read book, covering the entire range of living things, a renowned biologist lays the broad basis for understanding why animals behave as they do.

Index

11,173

591.5   Hirsch, S
H   Carl
        He and she

JUN 2 '77	DATE DUE		
Pac R			